Miniaturised Communications

a review of microforms

BERNARD J. S. WILLIAMS

The Library Association
London

The National Reprographic Centre for documentation
Hatfield

1970

Published by the Library Association,
7 Ridgmount Street, London, WC 1E 7AE

and The National Reprographic Centre for documentation,
Hatfield, The Hatfield Polytechnic, Hatfield, Herts
SBN: 85365 112 4

Based on a thesis accepted by
The Library Association for
Fellowship, 1969

Printed by LSG Printers Chronicle Building Waterside North Lincoln

CONTENTS

page number

INTRODUCTION

This review is concerned with the uses, applications and potentialities of microforms in communications systems. "Communications" is a sweeping term, but it is used here to refer to the overall field involving the storage, retrieval and dissemination (or publication) of information of a graphic or textual nature and the extent to which microforms can supplant or complement the conventional media (consisting mainly of books, periodicals, technical and scientific reports, manuals and catalogues). Certain specific forms of communication other than these have been excluded: all forms of business documents (exemplified by letters, invoices, accounts and records, such as personnel records) and engineering and architectural drawings and plans. Both of these groups —business records and engineering drawings—are major areas of microform application. In spite of the lack of systematic coverage their influence pervades the review since much of the hardware was produced primarily for these fields and was only adapted with varying success for the more general area with which the review is specifically concerned. They were excluded because they generally entail a different set of systems requirements. Furthermore, since the literature of each exceeds that of the field covered, it would not be practicable to encompass all in a review in depth.

The review is intended for the user and for those responsible for overall systems. It is not concerned with the minutiae of optics, silver halide or diazo chemistry or film transport mechanisms (indeed, few items relating to microfilm are), neither with the details of technical procedures such as developer bath temperatures and lens aberration testing.

The emphasis is on the state-of-the-art as it stands today although an earlier chapter cites some obvious primary and secondary sources relating to the history of the subject.

Finally, it is scarcely necessary to point out that the media which owe much of their development to the enormous increase in recorded knowledge and its associated problems are themselves the subject of a large and continuing literature.

The abstracts on which this review was based were collected and indexed at the National Reprographic Centre for documentation over a four year period. At the time the review went to press new abstracts were accumulating in the system maintained by the centre at a rate of several hundred per year. Current abstracts together with keyword indexes are published in the centre's quarterly bulletin. Accumulations together with a thesaurus of terms are published irregularly. Readers wishing to keep up to date with developments post dating this review are advised to use the NRCd abstracts service.

CHAPTER 1

THE TERMINOLOGY OF MICROREPRODUCTION

The terms used throughout this review and appearing in the glossary of terms (appendix 1) are taken, with exceptions indicated in the appended glossary, from the Glossary of terms published by the National Microfilm Association (USA) (1). This publication, now in its fourth edition and under the editorship of D. M. Avedon, is itself based on terms taken from a variety of United States national and government standards and from glossaries of professional organisations and other bodies. It contains over 400 terms (including trade names) which with a few minor exceptions ("book carriage" is preferred to "book holder", for example) fairly reflect both English usage and, if there is such a distinction, usage in England. The number of terms have increased over the editions, and definitions have changed in the light of modern practice (in the third edition, for example, "negative" is defined in terms of a tone reversal of the original; in the current, fourth edition the more pragmatic approach defining it in terms of light lines on a dark background has been adopted. In fact therefore an image with dark lines on a light background which was a tone reversal of the original would be a negative according to the earlier definition, a positive according to the later one).

British Standards referring to microforms define in total about 30 terms necessary for the interpretation of the standards (all are effectively compatible with those in Avedon's glossary). The preparation of a British standard glossary of terms is at present at an early stage of work under the auspices of the PHC 16 committee and in liaison with the committee responsible for producing a general list of terms in the documentation field.

The International Organisation for Standardisation (ISO) have produced two official recommendations (3 and 4). Both are very restricted in coverage—ISO R 260 (4) includes only twelve basic terms. Unfortunately, many of the ISO terms reflect neither common usage in English nor the practice in the Avedon glossary or official British standards. For example, British Standard 4187 (5) and Avedon (1) are in virtual agreement on the definition of microfiches in terms of a sheet of microfilm containing multiple micro-images in a grid pattern. However ISO R 260 uses the terms "Sheet microfilm" ("a transparent rectangular sheet on which is arranged a number of microcopies") and "Film microfiche" ("Sheet microfilm of smaller size as used for analytical or bibliographical index cards"). Leaving aside the question of undefined size differences implied by the ISO definitions, these are terms which have totally failed to find acceptance or use either officially or otherwise in English. Parallel definitions for micro-opaques according to ISO are "Sheet micro-opaque" and "Opaque microfiche". The latter to most English-speaking users is virtually a contradiction in terms.

In 1961 F. Luther reviewed the "language of Lilliput" for librarians in a series of seven articles (2).

H. W. Ballou (6), J. E. Crow (7) and D. M. Avedon (8) all plead the case for standardisation in terminology. Avedon relates how the various interpretations of the word "resolution" can lead to contractual misunderstandings. A discussion following a paper by Borden (9) provides an unintended demonstration of the confusion which can arise when the definition of "generation" is not well understood.

P. W. Howerton (10) makes some useful contributions to terminology but his suggestion that "Ultra micro-images" should be used for reduction ratios in excess of 1:35 looks an excessively low demarcation line now that many general purpose rotary cameras reach 1:45, while two proprietary microfiche systems, Microvue and PCMI, attain reductions of over 100 times (this latter figure perhaps now provides a more suitable threshhold). Howerton was writing in 1962.

CHAPTER 2

SOME HISTORICAL SOURCES

It is not the intention of this review to cover in detail the history of microforms, since this area has already been well covered in two previous reviews published in "The State-of-the-Library Art" series of Rutgers University (11 and 12) which deal respectively with the production of microforms and with reading devices in impressive detail. What follows is therefore a short review of some obvious sources.

F. Luther (13) gives a detailed account of the early history of microfilm 1839-1900. W. Browning (14) and L. L. Ardern (309, 310, 343) provide information on the British inventor of microfilm, John Benjamin Dancer. A. F. C. Pollard (15) has written a general account of miniature documents created by hand as well as by photographic means.

H. W. Ballou (16) outlines the development of the aperture card from its beginning in 1934, through its development during the 1939-1945 War, to the standards established by the United States Department of Defense which effectively provide the basis for all current aperture card based engineering drawing standards. It is interesting to note that what appears to be the original proposal for a type of aperture card made by Atherton Seidel in 1934 (17) envisaged it as a medium for disseminating technical papers to scientific workers. In fact the widely used and systematically standardised aperture card of today was developed as a medium for engineering drawings. Only recently in its "eight up" (8 document images on the 35 mm frame) has the aperture card begun to emerge as something akin to Seidel's concept. N. MacKay (311) has produced a useful short chronological account of the development of the aperture card. Published by the 3M Company, the book naturally emphasises this company's products.

It would be rash to speak of the "inventor" of the microfiche since this is one of the oldest microforms. What is certainly true is that the modern microfiche with its eye legible title strip and grid of micro-images has been in continuous use following developments in Germany and France just prior to World War 2. Dr. J. Goebel developed a step-and-repeat camera design in Germany and he describes his early work in a four-part article (18). At about the same time G. Cordonnier was using a 100 x 150 mm microfiche in France and brief details of both his and Goebel's work are given by J. Voskresenski (20).

E. P. Taubes (19) gives a brief history of microfilm as a business systems tool. De Sola's book (21), by reason of its early publication date (1944), is in itself now largely of historical significance and contains numerous pictures of contemporary equipment.

A common theme frequently appearing in innumerable articles and books sees microform applications in the past as being largely "inactive" —that is restricted to records likely to be little or even, in the case of security files, possibly never used, while many current and future applications are seen as "active" systems in which the microform is envisaged as a relatively heavily used record, sometimes indeed the only record. E. P. Taubes (19) considers "the modern period" began in 1928 when George McCarthy developed and exploited a camera for recording cheques and related documents in transit through banks and subsequently became president of what is now the Recordak Division of Kodak (a company which ever since has occupied a dominant position in the microforms industry). That such a trend exists and has existed for some time is easily observable, although less easily quantifiable. Yet paradoxically one of the earliest microfilm applications—that during the Franco-Prussian war in 1870 when microfilm carried by pigeons was used to convey messages into the beleaguered Paris—was clearly "active" in character. This frequently quoted episode is related in most detail by De Sola (21). The story of the escape of the microphotographer Renee Dagron from Paris in a balloon christened the "Niepce" together with his microfilming equipment and a companion, and of his journey through enemy territory disguised as a peasant woman with the apparatus hidden in wine barrels, is a frequently quoted episode in the early history of microforms.

The suggestion that modern microform history begins with the entry of Kodak into the market emphasises the interest of F. L. Hilton's "The First Kodak 40 Years" (331). Hilton traces the history of Kodak from McCarthy's 'Checkograph' cheque recorder through the emergence of 35 mm in 1935 to the "V" mail system of World War 2 and subsequently on to post-war developments. Numerous illustrations appear of early Kodak equipment.

CHAPTER 3

MICROFORM FORMATS AND MATERIALS

1 Formats

Microfilm formats fundamentally break down into roll formats and flat formats; within these categories the range of sizes, while in some cases unnecessarily wide, is effectively stabilised in the publishing, business records and engineering drawing fields. The field of combined search and store retrieval systems, however, contains a greater variety of sizes, particularly in flat formats, due, no doubt, to the need to fit the microform to the specific requirements of the retrieval equipment and the coding systems. Another factor is that the microforms used in such systems are machine as opposed to manually handled; a general purpose microform intended for manual handling cannot effectively go below a certain size commensurate with the size of and precision of the human hand. The single 35 mm x 42 mm frame size is being increasingly used in the engineering drawings and publishing fields but paradoxically the awkwardness of manually handling such a small unit accounts as much for its insertion into the 187 x 82 mm* punched card as does the facility for machine handling permitted by the latter.

From a dissemination systems point of view microforms are most usefully divided into respectively large and small capacity formats. Until recently large and small capacity formats equated respectively with roll and flat formats. Roll films in standard 30 metre (100 foot) lengths held upwards of 900 frames or pages while flat formats generally held no more than 100. The dissemination systems established during 1968 using the National Cash Register Company's PCMI ultra-high reduction ratio microfiches as a medium, each with a page capacity of up to 3,200 pages on international A6 size microfiches, have changed the situation as shown in figure 1 overleaf:

* Nominally $7\frac{1}{4}$ x $3\frac{1}{4}$ inches—the size of an obsolete United States dollar bill.

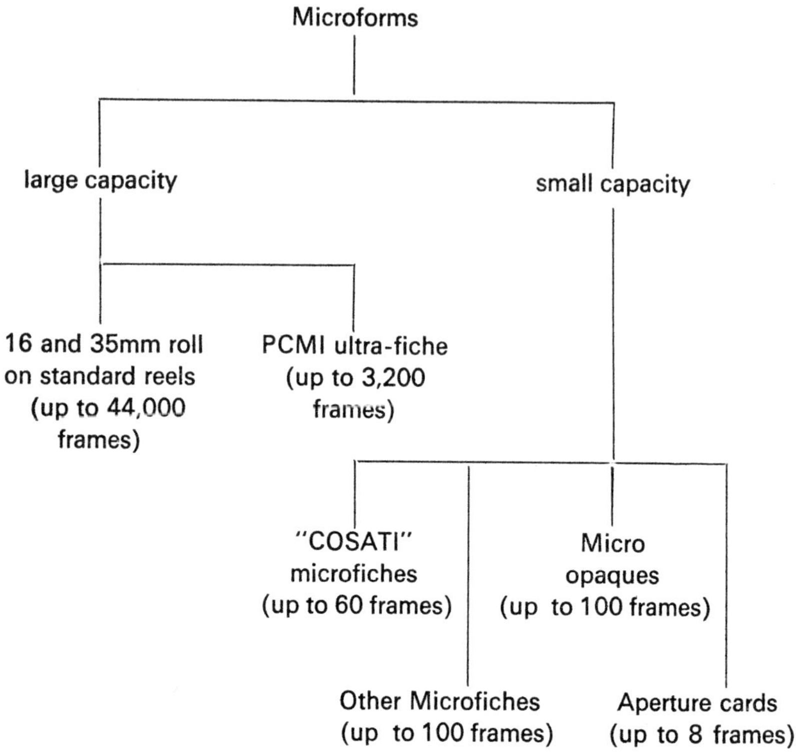

fig. 1 *Microforms divided into capacity classes; figures quoted are the generally established upper limit. Recent advances have raised the upper limit of 35mm to 44,000 frames.*

A further distinction is that between external and internal format. The former is related to the overall dimensions of the medium, the latter to the dimensions, orientation and layout of the frames on the medium. In the use of 35 mm roll film (external format) standards permit a variety of frame sizes and orientations (internal format); the National Microfilm Association (USA) microfiche standard (69) permits (among other options) the A6 microfiche (external format) with two ranges of frame size giving total capacities of 60 and 98 frame spaces (internal format). At an extreme it can be said that the PCMI microfiche adheres to the A6 external format but is unique in using an internal format giving up to 3,200 pages.

The modes of applications of the various forms will be examined in subsequent chapters.

R. Verry and G. H. Wright review the various microform formats in chapters two to seven of their book "Microcopying methods" (56) as does also J. L. Kish in "Microfilm for Business" (57). G. C. Baker (58) in reviewing formats draws an analogy between roll forms and books where pages are locked into order, and microfiches and loose leaf binders where they are not; he includes the ultra-high reduction ratio microfiche systems, such as PCMI, in the former group. B. J. S. Williams (59) reviews the status of microforms with specific reference to the library field.

2 Materials for Micro-Recording and Microduplicating

Materials in current common use for microrecording and microduplicating are silver halide, diazo and vesicular (or Kalvar) films, all of which are available in a wide variety of flat and roll formats. Silver halide is still the dominant medium for original recording; it is also used for microduplicating, especially in those areas where archival quality is required for the duplicate film (that is largely in some segments of the library and publishing fields). Where archival quality is not a requirement* and particularly where rapid 'on demand' microduplication is needed, diazo and Kalvar have largely replaced silver halide since they possess important advantages in that they can be handled in ambient light (both are sensitive to light in the ultra-violet range only) and are daylight processed by heat only or, in the case of diazo, by heat plus ammonia. They (particularly diazo) are used considerably in technical drawing systems for duplicating aperture cards, in the micropublishing field for the duplication of technical reports on microfiches and, to a more limited extent, in the business records field (more limited because the 16 mm rotary cameras usually used in business records are normally capable of simultaneous recording onto two silver halide films; only in systems requiring more than two films is there therefore any requirement for microduplication).

However, British (46) and Japanese equipment exists for direct microrecording onto Kalvar thus bringing the advantages of daylight handling and instant processing into microrecording in addition to microduplicating. (See summary in figure 2 over page.)

* There is a lack of objective information on the archival qualities of diazo and Kalvar and on the processing methods which might tend to establish such qualities. It is the lack of such information rather than positive information to the contrary which tends to mitigate against their use for archival purposes. Kalvar in particular looks potentially an archival material.

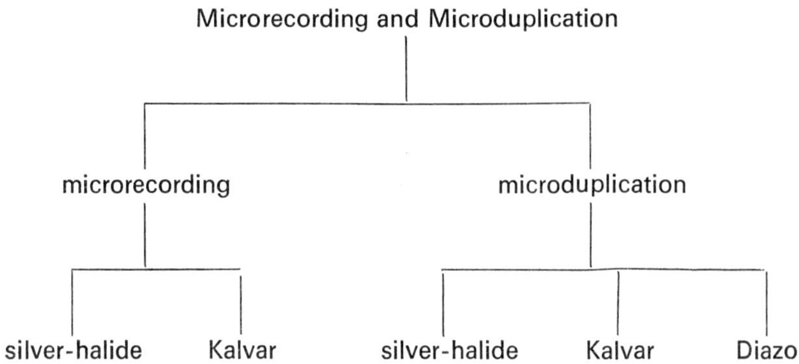

fig. 2 *The major processes of recording and duplication; Kalvar as a recording process is used only on certain new or prototype equipment.*

These represent the major processes available for microrecording and duplicating. Other new recording processes exist. The use of magnetic tape is being promoted by the Ampex Corporation (248-250); document images are recorded in diagonal tracks across a magnetic tape and it functions as both an original recording medium and, of course, exploits the well established magnetic tape facility for producing copy tapes (for further details see the chapter on information retrieval).

Other processes such as micro xerographic recording (159), xerographic frost imaging (54-5) and thermoplastic recording (52) have been in a developmental stage for periods often exceeding five years and, while technical descriptions of the processes are available, it is difficult to assess their practical and economic viability. Clearly, however, problems relating to at least one of these factors must account for their non-appearance as yet as working systems.

A technical review of materials for microrecording appears in chapter two of G. W. W. Stevens' "Microphotography" (280). The American management consultants Sharpe and Oughton, of Chicago, have reviewed the field (53) and so has P. Scott (40) in a brief survey. W. R. Hawken provides a most comprehensive and detailed survey in his "Copying methods manual" (23).

Silver halide film

The silver halide process is the basic method used in all types of photography and the basic physics of the process are outlined in countless sources. Silver halide microfilms use emulsions developed specifically to match the required characteristics for microrecording documents. The ability to record the detail with high resolution is the major requirement. Most microfilms possess a high contrast ratio (ideal for line or text work but less so for tone illustrations); some include anti-halation undercoats intended to eliminate the impairment of resolution resulting from the scattering of light rays through the film base. Most authors tend to take knowledge of the basic silver halide processes as read but W. R. Hawken (23) covers it and G. W. W. Stevens (280) covers both technical factors and the development of silver emulsions. C. P. Yerkes summarises the essential requirements (22).

Much of the technical emphasis in microform literature on the process relates to its archival qualities. A number of standards specifying the requirements for archival microfilm are reviewed in the chapter on Standardisation but most of the fundamental research on blemish formation has been carried out at the U.S. National Bureau of Standards (24-27, 275). The mechanism of the process which lead to degradation are, in some cases, still not fully understood but many authorities have evolved empirical methods to insure that information recorded on microforms is not lost through ageing or degrading of the micro-image. The U.S. Navy, for example (283), recommends: (1) The avoidance of unnecessarily high film densities (2) Careful processing including the addition of potassium iodide to the fixing solution and thorough washing (3) The avoidance of paper, string, adhesive tape or rubber bands to bind roll film (4) The use of sealed containers made out of inert materials (5) Correct storage environment (6) Careful handling (7) The use of microduplicates for working purposes (8) Inspection every two to three years and the production of a microduplicate if trouble is encountered.

A promising method for considerably improving the stability of silver micro-images is described by R. W. Henn and B. D. Mack (29) and effectively consists of the displacement of silver atoms by those of gold. The authors point out that, while silver is relatively stable and that many good negatives over 100 years old exist, it can react with reagents such as ozone and peroxide; gold, however, is a much less reactive metal.

Wear and tear is not strictly related very closely to archival quality and all authorities advise against the use of original negatives for working purposes, but it is a factor in the life of a working microduplicate and the question is reported on in detail by W. S. Suydam and A. G. Skove (281). A surprising result of tests carried out by these two authors showed that films processed without a hardener in the fixing bath were more scratch resistant than those in which a hardener was present. The question of extending the life of films by coatings is examined by G. T. Piez (28) who found that none of the eight proprietary coatings tested produced any overall improvement in scratch resistance. At present the problems of wear and tear would seem mainly to reside in roll film which in normal use may be driven through reader transport systems at speeds of up to 10 feet per second, but increasing trends towards mechanically sorting may produce similar problems for flat forms.

An interesting recent silver halide development from the Eastman Kodak company is described by H. J. Fromm and S. C. Insalaco (30); this is a negative working silver halide film for microduplicating. Normal silver halide films are sign reversing; the first generation or camera film is a negative, a second generation silver halide microduplicate would normally be a positive. The new film referred to by Eastman Kodak as "direct duplicating silver halide film type SO-156" is non-sign reversing and produces, therefore, negative microduplicates from negative films and positive microduplicates from positives. It is claimed to have a finer grain than other microduplicating films, is of relatively low contrast and can be exposed in existing contact printers with minor modifications (it is not stated whether the modifications would preclude the use of the unit for conventional films). It can be processed in "some" of the standard silver halide processors using solutions the same as for conventional Kodak films. No information on the basic physics of the new emulsion are given either by Fromm and Isalaco or in the official press release from Eastman Kodak (31).

It is worth examining the potential area of applications for the new film; the facility to go from a negative to a positive (or vice versa) is provided by conventional silver halide and by Kalvar; from a negative to a negative or positive to a positive by diazo or by the new Kodak direct duplicating film. Silver halide as a duplicating medium is economically competitive with both Kalvar and Diazo for roll-to-roll copying and with both also for microfiche duplication (although it is less convenient for "on demand" duplication). Additionally, it tends to be preferred (rightly or wrongly) where archival quality is a requirement (usually in the field of micro-publishing for libraries). The new film caters ideally, therefore, for those areas where negative distribution microduplicates are required which are archivally permanent.

Diazo

Diazo is already in very wide use, particularly in aperture and microfiche systems as a microduplication medium and a range of roll-to-roll, aperture card-to-aperture card and microfiche-to-microfiche microduplication devices are available. Diazo film is relatively slow and is sensitised by means of diazonium salts. Diazonium salts are organic chemicals which, under certain circumstances, are able to join with other organic chemicals to form dyes. The diazonium salts are sensitive to light in the ultraviolet; if diazo film is processed without exposure to light it will emerge darkened over its entire surface. Where, however, it is placed in contact with an original film, the light passes through the clear areas of the original and renders the diazonium salts exposed inert—those non-exposed areas protected by the dark areas of the original film will darken on processing; thus diazo is a non-sign reversal medium. Since normal daylight contains a relatively low level of ultraviolet, unexposed diazo film can be handled in daylight. Diazo film normally contains a coupler and is processed by passing it through ammonia vapour. The vapour permits the coupler to interact with the diazonium salts and to produce an image. It is also technically possible to produce diazo processed by heat alone. A. J. O. Axford (32) gives a good technical account of the process and possible future developments. C. H. Benbrook (33) and G. W. Smith (34) outline its characteristics as a microfilm duplicating medium while W. R. Hawken (23) covers the use of diazo for both micro and full sized duplicating. J. W. Boone and H. S. Todd (35) also cover diazo characteristics and draw attention to the need to evolve standard techniques to measure the characteristics, particularly density, speed, shelf life, archival life and resolution. The techniques for measuring and specifying diazo characteristics, relatively well established for silver halide, have been engaging the attention of standards committees for some years. The appearance in 1968 of an American Federal Standard (Federal Standard L-F – 315b) therefore seems a significant step forward. J. P. Deley and J. S. Dyer (36), in a review of the standard, state that it covers ammonia developed diazo film in 16 to 70 mm widths. It is said to specify a density requirement of 1.45 to 0.11 on a Macbeth Quanta Log Densitometer using a Wratten 93 filter. Methods and specifications for speed rating, accelerated aging, actinic transmission and resolution are also covered.

Diazo microduplication in engineering drawing systems is covered by K. B. Kasik (37) and by C. E. Nelson (284) while its general significance for microduplication is presented in the form of questions and answers (38) where the points that it is less susceptible to damage and scratching than silver halide are brought out. An evaluation report on a proprietary reader published by the National Reprographic Centre for documentation (39) also reveals that diazo film is less liable to damage from heat when in a reader than is silver halide film. The greatest drawback of diazo appears to be uncertainty about its permanence and it is seldom used where archival quality is a requirement. W. R. Hawken (23) indicates that permanence is "limited" but not "poor". C. E. Nelson (284) notes that diazo films kept away from ultraviolet light remained unchanged over a ten year period and he states that accelerated ageing tests indicate a potential life of at least 50 years.

Kalvar or vesicular film

Kalvar is the registered trade name of the Kalvar Corporation for a type of vesicular film. No doubt because Kalvar is the only vesicular film at present used in micrographics, the shorter trade name is almost invariably used in preference to the lengthier non-trade term. Kalvar in conventional systems is restricted to microduplicating (but developments involving its use for microrecording are covered in the next section). Kalvar as a process is closely related to diazo; like diazo the process is based upon the sensitivity of diazonium compounds to light in the ultraviolet. In the case of Kalvar, however, the light sensitive substance is suspended in a plastic layer; on exposure to ultraviolet light the diazonium salt decomposes to give off nitrogen in the form of tiny bubbles or vesicles; on the application of heat, or by light alone for type 80 Kalvar (282), the plastic becomes soft and the vesicles convert into permanent distortions. While the unaffected parts of the plastic remain fully transparent, the vesicles act as light scattering centres and thus form the micro-image. Since the latent image is formed where the Kalvar is exposed to light (as opposed to diazo in which it is formed where protected from light), Kalvar is normally a reversal process. Finally, to achieve comparative permanence it is necessary to "fix" it by destroying the light sensitive compounds in the previously unexposed areas. This is done by exposing the entire film to ultraviolet light for roughly four times the length of the original exposure In this case no subsequent heat is applied, the gases formed simply seeping away leaving de-sensitized transparent areas. While, at least to the layman, diazo and silver images appear substantially the same on a casual visual examination, the Kalvar image is quite distinctive with typically a salmony-whitish appearance. Its characteristics as a projected image are substantially unaltered, however. For microduplication purposes Kalvar can be processed on the same apparatus as diazo; the essential differences being the use of heat only for Kalvar (the lack of ammonia fumes is an advantage of Kalvar). This permits some flexibility in "on demand" microduplication; assuming a master file of negatives the requestor can be supplied optionally with negative diazo or positive Kalvar microduplicates*. In fact the main application for Kalvar has been in engineering drawing systems using projection dyeline print out;

* *A study undertaken at the National Reprographic Centre for documentation during 1969 indicated that processing temperature needed far finer control when processing Kalvar. Equipment evolved primarily for diazo processing might therefore fail to give optimum results with Kalvar.*

since projection dyeline is a non-sign reversal print out process, a positive micro-image is required to obtain a positive print out and these are usually obtained from the original negative micro-image by means of an intermediate Kalvar microduplicate.

Until recently Kalvar was purely a microduplication medium but a British company has produced a camera for recording onto Kalvar microfiches and aperture cards. There is less certain news of similar cameras under development in Japan and in the U.S.A. Further details of these developments appear in the section dealing with unconventional recording processes.

W. R. Hawken (23) surveys the overall attributes of Kalvar. P. Scott (40) and J. Dugan (41) also cover it briefly in their respective surveys of media and materials. Detailed monographs on the Kalvar process have been produced by E. E. Sandlin and M. G. Anderson (42), by M. E. Rabedeau (43), by R. T. Nieset (44) and by Caps Consultants (45). Its function particularly in engineering drawing systems is covered in (46) and by T. Wilson in (47). Kalvar, like diazo, suffers from the fact that techniques and specifications for establishing its characteristics lag behind those which exist for silver halide. R. M. Lindquist and M. E. Rabedeau (48) have written in detail on instrumentation for standardised testing of Kalvar films. N. T. Notley (282) describes how the newest Kalvar, type 80, is processed not by heat but by light alone in a process lasting less than one milli-second. J. P. Goodwald (49) outlines a retrieval device for maps: the maps are microrecorded onto 35 mm or 70 mm silver halide and the images with the addition of an optical binary location code, are transferred to a Kalvar scroll 17inches wide and 400 feet long. Any map can be retrieved and displayed in an average of 20 seconds using a scan rate of 12,000 pages per second. Resolution exceeds 144 lines per millimetre; output apart from the screen image can be by microduplication onto a Kalvar aperture card.

Unconventional microrecording processes

1 Kalvar

The possibility of bringing the daylight handling and instant dry processing of Kalvar to the microrecording operation itself clearly opens up new fields for microform systems since it makes the "on demand" micro-recorder a practical proposition. The first attempt at meeting such a concept was the announcement in 1965 of a design by W. J. Pfaff (50) but nothing further on this particular design has been published. In Japan the Canon Company have marketed a Kalvar aperture card camera; no reports on this device in operation are available.

In the United Kingdom Caps Research supported by a grant from the National Research and Development Corporation have developed a Kalvar microfiche camera. Caps envisage the camera as the cornerstone of a "MIDAS" (micro-image data addition system) (146). The system demonstrates the advantages of the Kalvar process for microrecording. The use of "MIDAS" in an office or library situation would entail the use of Kalvar microfiches on which each image is exposed and processed individually. Kalvar is slower than silver halide and inevitably the exposure time is much longer, but important compensations lie in the abilities to handle in the daylight and to flash develop the exposed frame and thus produce a processed micro-image within seconds of the recording operation. Unused parts of the microfiches can have further images recorded onto them within the shelf life of the unexposed Kalvar. In an office, a file could be updated by the addition of further data; in a library the user could add further material to that already recorded on the same microfiche, but the unused areas, however, should not be unreasonably exposed to ambient ultraviolet light (a protective envelope is used) or to such light in reader or other projection devices.

Given that the new equipment performs adequately and the capital and running costs are reasonable, the process appears extremely promising but much work will need to be done on the establishment of fundamental optical and physical characteristics and methods of measuring them so that factors such as archival quality can be as well assured for Kalvar as they already are for silver halide. The first Caps Kalvar camera for field use was supplied to the information department of the Gas Council, London, in Autumn, 1969.

2 Xerography

The Bell and Howell micro-xerographic camera (159) was a device with somewhat similar systems advantages to Kalvar cameras. The development of the device was funded by a grant from the Council on Library Resources and a field trial camera was for a time in service at the John Crerar Library, University of Illinois. While the relative insensitivity to normal ambient light of Kalvar is a useful attribute, the microxerographic processes characteristics which take the same attribute even further; the transparent material upon which the recording is made is completely insensitive until it receives a corona charge inside the camera. Unexposed areas are therefore completely inert and the microfiche can be used without the restraints imposed by Kalvar material. Additionally, for what it is worth, the camera could record onto opaques as well as transparencies. As with Kalvar, the exposure time would have been lengthy relative to silver halide.

All of this, unfortunately, is negated by the fact that since the announcement of the project in 1962 no further information on progress has been published and a direct enquiry failed to produce any positive response. Clearly in view of the time lapse some problems, either economic, technical or legal, have arisen and to that extent the ultimate outcome must be in doubt. A U.S. patent (348) was taken out by Bell and Howell in 1964.

3 Thermoplastic Recording and Frost Xerography

Thermoplastic recording and Frost xerography are two processes with some points in common and under development respectively by the General Electric Co. and the Xerox Corporation in the U.S.A.

J. G. Levinthal (52) describes the thermoplastic recording process. Thermoplastics are defined as substances which are soft and pliable when heated and which retain their shape on cooling. In the process a thermoplastic layer is laminated onto an electrically conductive base. An electron gun similar to those in television sets is used to "write" the image on the film. On heating, the electrons deposited on the surface forming a latent image are attracted towards the opposite charge in the conducting layer. This deforms the material and the resultant deformations become light scattering rather than light transmitting, and so form an image. On cooling, the deformations become permanent. Perhaps the most significant potential advantage is that the image is erasable and subsequently re-usable since thermoplastics can be repeatedly heated, formed, deformed on exposure and cooled. Good resolution is also claimed. Disadvantages include a surface which is liable to further deformation by scratching and the fact that cathode ray tube recorders are bulky and "moderately expensive". The market consultants, Sharpe & Oughton, of Chicago, state (53) that the process is in the development stage and that its application to microform systems is difficult to assess but it would certainly not be applicable to small users. A U.S. patent (349) taken out by General Electric gives details of the film tape, recording and erasing operations and of the exposing and reading stations.

Details of Frost xerography are given in papers by R. W. Gundlach (54) and C. J. Claus and W. A. Sullivan (55). Frost xerography differs from conventional xerographic processes mainly at the development stage. The thermoplastic surface is electrically charged; on exposure to light a variable charge pattern is formed on the surface and the charged areas of the heat softened plastic form microscopic depressions and ridges with light scattering qualities similar to those of fine grain frost (hence the name). As in the G.E.C. thermoplastic recording process, the micro-image is erasable and re-usable. Resolution of at least 150 lines per millimetre is claimed and the process is said to be fast, versatile and simple. Disadvantages include a greater sensitivity to abrasion than conventional microfilm (it is suggested that this could be overcome by laminating a protective layer over the surface but presumably only at the cost of losing the erasability feature), inability to contact print and the fact that prolonged exposure to heat about 150°F would destroy the image. The price of recording apparatus is projected as cheaper than a conventional camera/processor combination.

The only reasonable conclusion from all of these developments involving Kalvar cameras, microxerography, xerographic frost imaging and thermoplastic recording is that an enormous amount of development effort will appear to have been wasted if some form of instant dry microrecording process does not come into use in the next five years.

4 Magnetic tape

It is also possible to record and microduplicate micro-images in the form of tracks across magnetic tape. The one available system, the Ampex Corporation's Videotape system, constitutes a complete retrieval system and is reviewed in the chapter on information retrieval.

5 Photochromism

In the strict sense photochromic substances are not used for producing original microrecordings, only for producing a further reduction from an existing micro-image.

The exploitation of photochromics for micro-image purposes has been solely the work of the National Cash Register Company through PCMI (Photochromic micro-image) system. The process is described by A. S. Tauber and W. C. Myers (164) of NCR and in commendable detail by W. C. Myers in an official NCR booklet (285). Photochromic compounds exhibit colour changes in response to radiant energy in the visible or near visible portions of the spectrum. The coatings developed by NCR are claimed to be completely grain free and therefore possess inherently high resolution capabilities. On exposure the image becomes instantly visible and no processing is required. The coatings are reversible; the image can be erased by exposure to light in a different wavelength and subsequently replaced by another image. Photochromic images are unstable and have only a short life at normal temperatures; in practice, as detailed below, complete photochromic masters are contact printed onto silver halide sub-masters on completion.

In operation the PCMI system permits reductions of 100 to 150 times giving a capacity of up to 3,200 pages on an A6 microfiche. Original material is initially recorded onto 35mm silver halide microfilm at a normal reduction of typically 10x. A specification (286) for this work, normally not done by NCR, has been issued. The 35mm image is then transferred at a further reduction of 10–15x onto the photochromic master using a PCMI recorder. The operator inspects each image shortly after it is made and erases and re-records where any errors or sub-standard images are found. When a complete master of up to 3,200 images has been created, it is contact printed onto a high resolution silver halide master which, in turn, is used to produce further silver halide contact prints for dissemination. Each is laminated to protect the image from damage.

The process is essentially a publication process unsuited to one-off or short run situations. Total cost of creating a PCMI master is approximately £350 (including the original 35 mm recording) while dissemination duplicates cost about ten shillings each. PCMI recording is done under contract by NCR. PCMI readers are normally rented but thought to cost about £200.

As a publishing method the process appears to offer substantial economies over conventional publication. It is reported to have been adopted for manuals by the Ford Motor Co. (U.S.A.) and in Britain is being used for the Technical Information on Microfilm (TIM) product information service (154, 287) and by the British Leyland Motor Corporation for distributing parts lists to their agents (313).

"RS" Process (radiation sensitive)

The "RS" process has been developed by the Itek Corporation (U.S.A.). According to a report from the management consultants, Sharp and Oughton (53), it is a process in which an agent making the basic material photo-sensitive is added just prior to exposure. Exposure is to light in the ultraviolet, processing is wet. K. G. Clark (288) states that it is based on the fact that certain radiation sensitive materials (metal oxides or metal sulphides) retain a latent image on exposure to actinic light. The latent image is converted by photographic development using silver or other metal ions or organic dyes such as methylene blue. The "RS" process is used in a new series of reader printers from Itek and duplicate microfilm produced by the process was distributed at a Royal Photographic Society conference in Oxford in 1969. The possibilities of original recording onto "RS" film remain to be reported on.

CHAPTER 4

LIBRARY MICROFORM SYSTEMS

Introduction

The literature on microform applications in the library and documentation fields presents to the researcher a series of paradoxes. On the one hand it can appear to be a minor field of application for microforms; it is clear from the reviews appearing in the following section, for example, that equipment manufacturers in general do not, or at least have not, found the market sufficiently large to produce much equipment specifically for it. Librarians themselves have often seemed to allocate a comparatively minor role to microforms in library systems; for example, C. F. Scott, of the University of London, stated in 1967 (119) that it was the library's policy not to purchase microforms unless no alternative was available. On the other hand, when examining the potential of microform media as projected by authorities such as L. B. Heilprin, of the Council on Library Resources (67) and P. Scott, of the Massachusetts Institute of Technology (61), and the actuality of the publications programme of the United States Government, together with the proposals of numerous commercial publishers, it becomes clear that the combined library and publishing fields (which obviously interrelate very closely) really appear to be on the brink of a very rapid expansion in the use of miniaturised media to a point where they could become commonplace as a method of textual and graphical communication. How far such a trend would go is a matter for speculation; it is underway in the technical and scientific fields and, through the activities of organisations such as the Educational Resources Information Center (ERIC) in the U.S.A., it has moved into the education area. These are fields where reading is done for a purpose; the ultimate in microforms acceptance would see their use for recreational reading.

However, it will be shown in the following paragraphs that microforms have tended to fall short of gaining full acceptance for continuous reading tasks and that such acceptance depends on improved standards in resolution and quality control, in the performance of readers and reader-printers and in the systems established by libraries.

In the past improvements have been slow in coming, largely because standards were generally adequate only for the business records field where the major market lay. It was difficult to persuade manufacturers and micro-publishers that the improvements needed to make the continuous reading of micro-images of originals containing fine detail acceptable to users were likely to be economically justified. It must be hoped that, under the influence of the major microform publishing programmes, this situation will change quickly enough for microforms to add acceptability for continuous reading to their established attributes of space savings, accessibility and low cost dissemination and publishing.

The current state of library microtext applications

"Scientists and scholars generally are very much like a group of small boys playing at marbles while the circus went by . . . now (it) has gone into the tent they are going to have to step right up and buy the price of admission." (Vernon Tate)

Vernon Tate's picturesque analogy on the state of microforms applications in libraries was made in 1950 (60). In 1970 the fairest assessment would be that the world of documentation is indeed beginning to reach into its pocket to find out whether it has the price of admission or whether indeed there remains any alternative.

Failures in library systems

That there has been a failure to exploit the potential of microforms is a widely supported thesis. P. Scott (61) sees it as a failure in systems development (he defines "system" as the complete answer to a need). Scott points out that the development of commercial microfilm applications has been a matter of careful analysis of specific requirements followed by the development of specific equipment. Libraries, however, are forced to adapt existing equipment and to reshape alien systems. R. R. Dickison (62) saw the failure as mainly related to two causes: lack of standardisation and user resistance. The former was related mainly to roll film which was found in three sizes (16, 35 and 70 mm), perforated or unperforated, negative or positive with reductions of anything from 8 to 30 times. User resistance arose from the need to visit a library to use a reader, in the difficulty of threading a roll film reader and then in locating the required image. He sees, however, at least some solutions in the use of cassette loading, which he considers will soon make an impact as great as that of the microfiche, and in the various systems for rapid frame location now available. Dickison considers the failure of micro-opaques to achieve the exciting possibilities forecast by Fremont Rider in 1944 in "The Scholar and the future of the research library" (63) lay in many cases in inadequate quality control, but above all in the failure to devise an acceptable reader-printer for micro-opaques—"all you could do with a microcard was read it, if you were lucky". He goes on to state that the situation in regard to microfiches appears promising, the microfiche is already standardised, simple desk-top readers costing below $100 are already available, and that a user survey carried out by the Special Libraries Association (U.S.A.) (65) indicated that, with some reservations about quality, user resistance appeared to be disappearing.

A Unesco survey published as long ago as 1951 (131) concluded that standardisation was one of the root causes restricting the use of microcopying: "The main reason why the process has not been more widely adopted lies in the fact that the development of equipment and techniques had proceeded independently in different countries, and consequently a wide range of equipment has been produced which is not interchangeable. Neither the manufacturer nor the user is inclined to develop the equipment further and to extend its use until some measure of standardisation is introduced."

B. J. S. Williams and G. H. Wright (66) also considered the loading of roll film or reels (a "frustrating and annoying process") to be a contributing factor in user resistance to roll films and, like Dickison, put forward a plea for the use of cassette loading. They gave other reasons for the failure to exploit microforms in libraries as: (1) Inadequate financial resources of libraries leading to low level demand and conseqent failure to produce equipment specifically for libraries; (2) Conservatism of British librarians; (3) Inadequacies in equipment; (4) Lack of user education in the potential of microform systems; (5) Absence until recently (the paper appeared in 1967) of a major microform based publishing programme.

In a discussion following a paper by S. N. Alexander and F. C. Rose (141), Vosper drew a similar conclusion to point (1) above in reminding the audience that any failure to follow the commercial world in the extend of microfilm applications was due to the fact that "risk" capital did not exist in the library world and that few libraries had adequate research and development funds. However, he went on to refute any suggestion that librarians had an attitude of resistance—on the contrary, he considered that there was a sense of urgency and need on this topic.

W. R. Hawken (68) considered again that the failure lay in the field of standardisation. His general thesis was that the diversity of film sizes, image sizes, image shapes and reductions had "erected imposing barriers to the effective use of microforms and to the development of inexpensive and efficient reading devices. The problems are even more acute where the need for hard copy must be met." The paper goes on to give an extremely detailed analysis of factors which have contributed to the situation. On the question of roll film Hawken notes that in other fields of use—specifically motion pictures and in amateur hand cameras—a very high degree of standardisation has been attained: "A motion picture made with American cameras can be shown to an audience in Africa on French made projectors." In early microfilming onto roll Hawken stated that some measure of standardisation did exist because adapted cine or hand cameras were used. But most significantly Hawken goes on to blame the present proliferation of sizes and reduction ratios onto a specific organisation, the Recordak division of the Eastman Kodak Company. Recordak cameras, he states, have largely dominated the field and virtually destroyed what standardisation existed by their flexibility—frame length could be varied at will, the head could be rotated to record the image across or along the film, reduction ratios and image sizes could be varied. All of these features permitted economies in the use of film. Later on, with the emergence of continuous enlarger printers such as the Xerox Copyflo, economics in the use of print paper added to the advantages of cameras flexible in operation, but all of these production advantages were bought at the price of increasing the problems in use. Ideally a microfilm reader for the products of such versatile cameras should be as versatile as the camera but would be almost as expensive as the camera itself as a result (the current Recordak MRD-2E, a popular camera for library use, costs £900 – £1,000 in Great Britain). Hawken goes on to say that most readers exhibit compromises in their compatability with camera versatility while reader-printers additionally exhibit further problems associated with limited print paper size and loss of sharpness which tends to send under-magnified prints towards —and sometimes over—the boundary of acceptable legibility.

On the question of microfiches, Hawken notes that while European produced microfiches have exhibited flexibility in the size image capacity and in the reduction ratios used, microfiches from the United States have tended to conform to the NMA and COSATI standards (69 and 64), which utilised a fixed frame size on a 105 x 148 mm microfiche with a maximum reduction of 1:20. He points out that these standards were intended to suit the characteristics of typewritten report material, but were increasingly being used for the finer detail of printed originals for which they were unsuitable. Hawken's key proposal lay in the establishment of a maximum image size and a maximum reduction ratio for all micro-media – this to be established on the basis of the internal characteristics (that is the fineness of detail) of original documents. The overall page size and even type size when expressed in points did not provide a suitable basis for the decision.

On the question of inadequate reader equipment for use in libraries, Hawken again has a great deal to say. He lists (100) common faults in reading equipment as:

(1) Lack of overall image sharpness. (2) Unsuitable screen size.

(3) Uneven illumination. (4) Insufficient illumination. (5) No control over illumination intensity. (6) Difficulty in loading. (7) Micro-image area too small. (8) Inadequate protection against scratching. (9) Insufficient control over illumination. (10) Excessive heat. (11) Inconvenient location of controls. (12) Poor screen angle. (13) Inadequate protection against light. (14) Maintenance difficulties. (15) Poor quality construction. (16) High cost.

The question of front versus rear projection readers and positive versus negative displays have long produced controversy among librarians and users. J. M. Judisch (351) reports on a research project carried out by H. R. S. Singer Inc. into this question. Reading speed and comprehension tests were carried out in all four modes. The results showed very little difference between the front and rear projection modes but significantly higher speed and comprehension rates when reading from positive as against negative displays. It is pointed out that the small difference between front and rear projection may be due to the particular display designs used and that further research is needed to clarify the issue. Further research is also needed into fatigue factors of the two modes. It is also considered that the positive versus negative results could have been influenced by the greater familiarity of the former to users.

Systems: Some current microform applications in libraries

The mainstream of general library microform applications are currently concerned with three roles: the saving of space, preservation, and the availability of rare, out-of-print and short run publications, documents and manuscripts.

Space savings

Fremont Rider (63), and numerous authors not directly concerned specifically with microforms, have drawn attention to the exponential growth rate of libraries. In the library, scientific and technical press there is constant reference, frequently supported by data in the form of graphs and statistics, to the enormous growth in the output of literature in these fields. It is outside the scope of this survey to review the literature relating to this phenomenon but, given the assumption that the growth does tally with much of the data quoted, it is clear that libraries, in their function as warehouses or stores of information, are increasingly concerned with the question of optimum utilisation of space. Rider points out that the more advanced the material is in a collection, the lower will be the per item rate of use over a given period. It is with the field of relatively inactive material that traditional microform applications in libraries have been mainly concerned (although literature reviewed later will tend to demonstrate an inversion of this concept) and, if the increase in selectivity (either by way of increased pressure of time on the individual user or by improved filtering methods typified by computer based selective dissemination of information SDI systems) effectively lowers the average acrivity rate per item, it will strengthen the traditional case for microforms in libraries.

S. N. Alexander and F. C. Rose (141) see six alternatives for copying with the burgeoning space requirements imposed on libraries by the continuing growth in publishing:

(1) Libraries maintain the same subject coverage but become more selective. (2) They restrict subject coverage and become more specialised. (3) Groups of libraries co-operate in interlending. (4) Some holdings are acquired on microform only. (5) To supplement (3) some form of facsimile transmission is used.

In short the choice is either one of reduction in coverage or in format size. The implications of this are reviewed in more detail on page 65.

Preservation

The use of microforms as a medium for the preservation of material in libraries and archives is an established application. While the long term preservation of books and manuscripts is generally of major concern only to national and depository libraries and specialist collections, the problem touches on all libraries concerned with the use of newspaper files, with the maintenance of special collections or with company or other organisational archives.

G. Williams, director of the Center for Research Libraries in Chicago, reports (70) on a detailed analysis of the problem followed by proposed solutions. He quotes the result of studies undertaken on behalf of the Council on Library Resources by W. J. Barrow during 1957/58 as showing that: "It seems probable that most library books printed in the first half of the twentieth century will be in an unusable condition in the next century". More specifically, the studies showed that of a sample of books printed in the U.S.A. during a 40-year period, 1900-1939, 40% were found to be so weak that given only moderate use they would be unusable by the general reader within another 20 years, and another 50% would be too weak for general use within 45 years. Williams stated that research has now produced a practical way to preserve deteriorating books by means of de-acidification techniques and that use of these techniques, together with environmental control, could extend the potential physical life of a book from 25 to 600 years. He goes on to state that it would cost only $2 more per volume to preserve the originals by these techniques and make a microfilm copy when specific books needed to be used than it would be to microfilm copies now and discard the originals completely. Based on this he makes two major recommendations: (1) That a central library should be established to accept from other libraries and physically preserve all books subject to the following conditions *(a)* it is best available physical example; *(b)* catalogue cards are supplied with it; *(c)* it is complete or the most complete available copy. (2) That the central library should have made a microfilm negative of any book required by another library and that it should lend a positive copy of the film free of charge; alternatively, that it should sell a positive copy or print-out at the cost of the copy alone (that is without adding any portion of the cost of making the original negative to the charge). Essentially, therefore, the proposals outlined by Williams envisaged microforms not as the primary preservation medium (which remains the original book) but as a medium for protecting originals from unnecessary wear and tear. There is no information available on the implementation of these proposals.

It is clear that microforms have two possible roles in preservation programmes: (1) As an alternative to attempting preservation of originals. (2) As a working copy to be used in lieu of originals, thus protecting them from wear and tear. Library practices in fact blurs this distinction. B. J. S. Williams reports (71) that the Library of Congress destroys originals of newspapers after microrecording while conversely he reports (72) that the Royal Library in The Hague microfilms newspapers for preservation purposes but continues to use the bound volumes for day to day working purposes. The Library of Congress practice on its "brittle books" preservation programme is reported to vary according to the condition of the original; only microrecorded originals that remain usable are retained. B. Babiczky (73) of the National Szechenyi Library in Budapest makes the point that allowing the condition of originals to degenerate too far lessens the practicability of making adequate microcopies. He, too, sees a valuable role for microcopies in protecting originals from wear and tear. It is probably a fair summary to state that while libraries would generally prefer to use microcopies in preservation programmes purely as a method for protecting originals from wear and tear, the inadequacy of their microrecording programme usually forces them willy-nilly into a situation where originals have gone beyond the point of physical preservation before they are microrecorded. It would follow paradoxically that the cause of the "preservation of originals" school would best be served by encouraging greater expenditure on microrecording.

The arguments in favour of the preservation of originals are set out by W. A. Jackson (74), who states categorically that no authoritative conclusions regarding a manuscript can be based on the examination of any known form of reproduction. He quotes several examples to prove this statement. His paper may be questioned when he expresses concern over the possible damage to rare books during microrecording without acknowledging at the same time that the existence of a microcopy will protect the original from unnecessary wear and tear by users less concerned with its physical form; furthermore, microrecording, unlike the usual alternatives, can be a once-only operation. That such damage may be inevitable if an adequate quality microcopy is to be obtained from closely bound originals with lines of text going into the gutter area cannot be denied, but most available copying processes would entail similar damage. The ethics of maintaining single copies inviolate but inaccessible to most potential users are in any case questionable.

A. Desmond (165), in describing the microfilming situation of the British Museum, states that since an Act of 1963 it has been permitted for the Museum to destroy material published after 1850 following microfilming—at present all foreign newspapers after 1850 are being so treated.

J. Aldern in a contribution entitled "Reproduction versus preservation; a reappraisal of the trend towards indiscriminate photoreproduction of rare books and manuscripts" (97) considers that widespread copying is a threat to the publishing and antique book trades (but it is very questionable whether the library profession should be concerned with bolstering book values through rarity and in any case whether microcopies substantially affect the values of originals). The author states that microfilm is "uncertain in character" and that it is no more lasting than "good" paper; he claims that the National Bureau of Standards " Inspection of Processed photographic film for ageing . . . " (98) sets a standard unlikely to be attained by libraries. He goes on to note that full sized copying processes are frequently the cause of damage to books and states that where there is a regular demand for copies of an original, microfilm is best since the negative can be retained as a master thereby protecting the original from unnecessary use. The question of supplying specific passages then becomes a problem, but he suggests that it may be reasonable to supply only the entire work in such cases since "if a fragment is worthwhile, so must be the entire work". He goes on to suggest that once a microfilm negative has been made, it is reasonable to refuse requests to copy direct from the original.

H. Leisinger (325) reports that questionnaires sent to American archivists reflected overwhelming support for expanded programmes of microfilm publication for both archival and manuscript material but quality control standards were critical and the need for improved bibliographic presentation expressed.

Micro storage as a method of saving storage costs

Sources quoted earlier have tended to indicate that there is, in some circumstances, little alternative to the use of micro documents in lieu of full sized documents due, respectively, to the rapid growth rate of libraries and to the requirements of preservation. Additionally, apart from the projections on growth rates of large libraries, there is the resultant practical problem summarised by an anonymous author (91) "when assessing the costs of space it is well to consider that very often factors leading to microfilming would otherwise have made new premises necessary . . . sometimes microfilm has to be seen as the price of the only possible solution".

This section is, however, concerned with the situation where the options of holding material in micro or full sized form remain open and the requirement is to base the choice purely on the relative costs of storage. It also disregards other factors, such as speed of access or limitations in use, which may arise when little used original material is relegated to a remote repository.

A particularly thorough survey of the relative costs in the U.S.A. was produced by Clapp and Jordan (92). The authors review the results of two projects carried out by consultants for the Council on Library Resources. They report in general that estimates made from time to time always come out in favour of retaining the originals unless additional considerations such as preservation, acquisition or the cost of binding are introduced. Reviewing the first of the studies—that carried out by Pritsker and Sadler in 1957 (93)—it is reported that results indicated that "on a cost basis, microfilm is feasible as a form of storage only if libraries are willing to accept a high reduction ratio, little or no inspection of the finished product, an image less perfect than could be obtained using a 35 mm planetary camera, and the destruction of the original text." However, it was decided that one particularly important question had not been answered by the study: "What would happen if the cost of the master negative should be shared among a number of subscribers to service copies?" Accordingly, the Council on Library Resources contracted with other consultants—this time Forbes and Waite, of Lexington, Massachusetts—to investigate this further question. Forbes and Waite considered four elements; the cost of making the master negative, the cost of service copies, the number of subscribers, comparative costs of constructing storage space for the originals and for the microfilms. They excluded: the overhead costs of the storage spaces involved, of servicing the collections, of changing catalogue entries, user costs and degree of satisfaction, questions of copyright. Their study was based on the cost of microfilming a hypothetical collection of 100,000 bound periodical volumes by the most economic method consistent with preserving all the printed information contained in the originals to a quality where it might be transmitted without material loss through three generations. From this "no loss of material information" came the consequence that coloured originals should be recorded on colour microfilm. Destruction of originals was to be permitted as part of the operation. In a carefully defined "typical case" (which defined average height of volumes, page density on shelves and similar factors) they found that microfilm could be successfully applied to the reduction of storage costs provided that five or more participants could be found. The number of participants would vary according to the difficulty of the originals and the amount of colour involved. They went on to say that considerations such as the cost of reading equipment and copyright excluded from the study, together with the work of organising such a project, would prove strong deterrents in undertaking it purely for space savings. However, the situation might change radically if high reduction ratio microfilming became practical. Also they noted that storage costs are possibly less important than other aspects of library work.

Effectively, therefore, the 1957 study showed that microfilm compared to full sized unbound storage could offer savings only under fairly severe restraints, while the later study showed that, given a move towards shared costs—virtually towards a republishing situation—microfilm could be viable without the need for restraints affecting usability. It is the shared costs, or publishing factor, which probably accounts for the discrepancies between the studies quoted above and the claims of microform publishers to be quoted below.

An anonymous article (94) produced in close association with University Microfilms, in Unesco Bulletin for Libraries, suggests that in a typical American library one square foot of floor space holds 15 books or 8 periodical volumes and that the average annual rental is about $2.50 (the British periodical "Economist" (95) gave the following figures for the U.K.: Central London 70s. per square foot; Glasgow, Newcastle, Manchester and Birmingham all about 20s.; suburban rates—London 25s., Glasgow nearly 20s., the remainder just over 10s.) On this basis annual storage cost for a bound periodical volume is 30c, while binding averages $3.50 for an 800-page periodical. Based on these figures the following graph shown in figure 3 was produced:

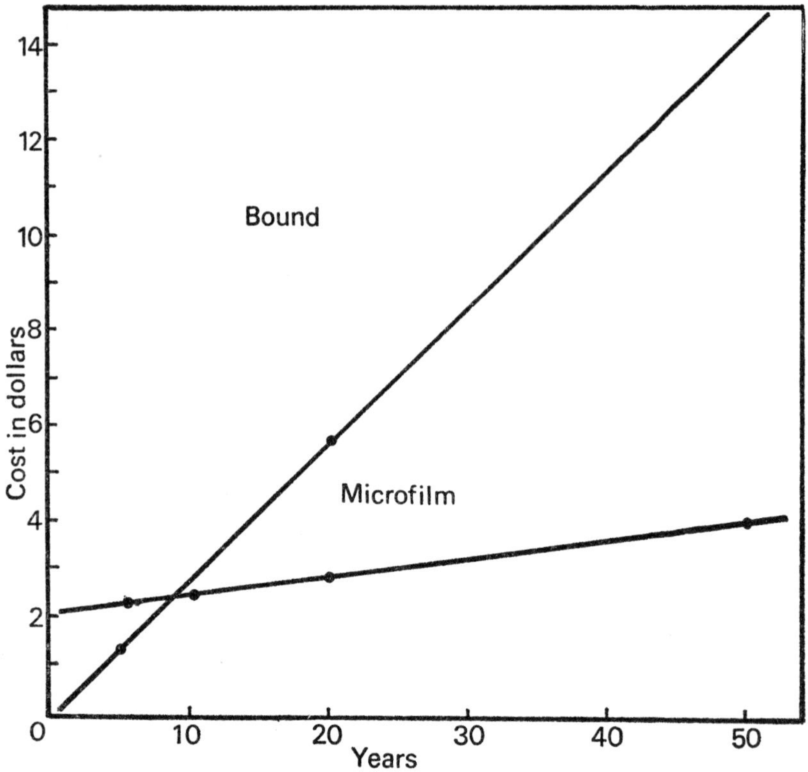

fig. 3 *Defunct periodical. Relative costs of storing a periodical volume of 800 pages in the usual bound form and on microfilm, for a varying number of years. The cost of storing the microfilm includes the original purchase price of the film.*

E. Power, of University of Microfilms Inc. (96) reproduced a graph showing that the storage and binding costs of newspaper files exceed the costs of microrecording and microform storage within about eight years. He goes on to state that an 800 page per year periodical, bound and stored over the same period, costs $112. Part of the reason is said to be the fact that storage costs of bound volumes are cumulative—after the first year the cost reaches 25c, after the second 75c, after the third $1.50 and so on.

General conclusions from the results given in the above sources would seem to be:

1 Microrecording of library material on a "one-off" basis purely as a method of reducing storage costs is unlikely to be justified.

2 On a shared cost basis, with a minimum of five subscribers and related to bound storage it may be viable.

3 The purchase of published microfilm is likely to lower storage costs as against bound volumes kept over a ten year period or longer, substantially.

4 Microfilm is unlikely to give lower costs over short term unbound storage.

Library catalogue and catalogue card production

There are two microform applications associated with library catalogues: a relatively long standing application employs microfilm as an intermediate for the production of catalogue cards while a significant recent application employs computer produced roll microfilm actually as a library catalogue.

Microfilm as an intermediate for catalogue card production

A. B. Veaner (101) describes the system of catalogue card production at Harvard University Library. Original cards were typed and micro-recorded onto 35mm roll using a Recordak MRD planetary camera. The processed film was then printed out on Xerox "Copyflo" electrostatic equipment. The original intention was to record onto 16mm roll and to print-out onto 5 inch web stock for guillotining to give 5 x 3 inch cards; however, the enlarger printer could not be modified and cards had to be recorded side-by-side on 35mm roll and printed out onto a 10 inch web. Cutting was automatic. Final print quality was found to be critical. The production rate including hole drilling and cutting was 5,000 cards per day, one million per year; this was thought to be well within the total capacity of the "Copyflo" and it was estimated that one machine on a one shift per day system could produce five million cards per year.

R. W. Loud (102) describes a substantially similar technique again using "Copyflo" print out. The author was connected to a commercial bureau (The General Microfilm Co., Cambridge, Massachusetts) offering the service on contract to libraries and claimed a 48-hour return service and a basic charge of 4c per card.

In 1968 the Information Dynamics Corporation, 80 Main Street, Reading, Massachusetts 01867, announced plans to publish the Library of Congress catalogue on microfiches. Each microfiche contains approximately 1,100 entries and the annual subscription embraces five years of the author and card number index plus weekly, monthly, quarterly and annual updating.

A computer produced catalogue

A radically new approach to library catalogue production is described by W. A. Kozumplik and R. T. Lange, of the Lockheed Missiles and Space Co. (103).

The system became operational in July, 1966, and is claimed by the authors to be "The most advanced, effectively used oriented catalogue system in operation today". The catalogue is computer processed and printed out via a Stromberg Carlson cathode ray tube computer output recorder onto 16mm roll. It consists of the following sections: 1 The basic catalogue. 2 A list of additions. 3 Updated open entry items. 4 Source authority lists. 5 Subject authority lists.

The catalogue is reprocessed quarterly; it has over one million entries covering both books and reports contained in 40 cassettes. Each cassette holds 1,800 pages of dual column text which previously filled 720 catalogue drawers. Each cassette is labelled as to contents and colour-coded to indicate which division of the catalogue it belongs to. The complete catalogue is updated quarterly in an operation which takes 10 days. Between the quarterly updatings users are kept informed of new items in a key-word-in-title (KWIT) index produced semi-monthly.

The authors claim a net saving over the conventional catalogue operation of $13,000 each year. The savings are said to result from the following factors: 1 No card filing costs. 2 No card catalogue costs. 3 200% space savings. The ability to duplicate the catalogue is considered an enormous bonus; another valuable "spin-off" is the ability to produce printed catalogues at exceptionally low cost. The micro-version has obtained good user acceptance from both scientists and librarians. If it did create objections, however, it would still be possible to print out 20 duplicates via a "Copyflo" enlarger printer at less than half the cost of copying full sized computer print-out and duplicating via offset ($409.60 as against $1,223.20).

A briefer description appears in Modern Office Procedures (318).

The progress of the system at Lockheeds will clearly be worth watching.

Bibliographic factors

There are two major aspects relating to the bibliography of microforms: 1 The overall status of microforms as bibliographic entities (this in turn raises questions on the legal deposit system and its applications to microforms, on tracing what is available on microform, and the avoidance of duplication in microrecording activities). 2 The cataloguing of microforms at individual library level.

The first question was the subject of a detailed study in 1964/65 carried out under the auspices of the Unesco International Advisory Committee on Bibliography, Documentation and Terminology by the Bibliotheque Nationale in Paris (104). The terms of reference were to "prepare a general study on how information on all types of microphotographic reproductions is secured and distributed", to look at the question of producing a bibliography of bibliographies, and finally to include "preliminary investigations into the possibility of drawing up lists of full length works or journals which should be micro-copied, reprinted or republished to meet the needs of developing libraries". The study encompassed 15 countries with the option of an extension (which apparently was taken up) to a further eight.

The study was carried out by means of a two-part questionnaire; the first part was concerned with bibliographical problems posed by microforms, the second with the compilation of lists of works or journals to be micro-recorded and republished for the needs of developing libraries. Recipients were asked to restrict their comments to microforms for sale commercially and to exclude catalogues of libraries even where published. The survey seems to have elicited about the normal level of response from recipients: of 185 sent out, 63 elicited replies but only 35 by way of completed questionnaires.

The conclusions were as follows:

1 Microcopies are definitely inadequately represented in non-commercial bibliographic publications (national bibliographies, special bibliographies and bibliographic journals); in fact only four national bibliographies do not specifically exclude microcopies. In view of this, the survey comments, it is not surprising that they are frequently overlooked in special bibliographies.

2 Scientific periodicals seldom mention microcopies. The survey considered this more surprising since periodical publishers ought to be directly informed by the microform publishers' press services, but the situation may be due to the fact that catalogues only are sent out and not review copies.

3 Remedies were suggested only by the best equipped countries (notably Italy, The Netherlands, Great Britain). Britain suggested that the Council for Microphotography and Document Reproduction (now the Microfilm Association of Great Britain) should act as a dissemination agency.

Other organisations suggested a union catalogue approach while the Central National Library in Florence recommended legal deposit enabling routine entry into national bibliographies. It was noted that, even in countries where legal deposit of reprints is a requirement, microcopies seem to have evaded the system. The survey considered this to be due to "the private nature of the operation" and the small number of copies produced—where only one copy was made, the requirement to deposit a further one could be unduly expensive. The survey went on to query the grounds for legal deposit when an item appeared in a microform publishers' catalogue on a speculative basis (i.e. when a microrecording is only made if an adequate number of orders are received—a common practice among smaller micro publishers). It went on to note that the American solution to these problems was to be the establishment of a central register of microform masters at the Library of Congress.

4 There were many recommendations on .the standardisation of cataloguing and production methods. It was pointed out on the question of archival quality that preservation of conventional publications was assisted by the wide dissemination, but where it was relatively limited, as with microforms, great onus was placed on the possessor of the unique master negative. This required permanent and reliable organisations.

5 No particular preference emerged on the choice of microfilm format.

6 Most organisations considered that lists of items for microrecording would be feasible at national or international level—exceptions to this view were expressed by the National Library of Scotland and the library of the Schweizerisches Sozialarchiv (Switzerland) who both considered that such lists would not be feasible bearing in mind the diversity of libraries involved. It was considered significant that the U.S.A. as the biggest user of microforms thought a programme necessary and urgent. Most countries selected their national library as the most appropriate co-ordinating body, but in Britain, Aslib and the Standing Conference of National and University Libraries were proposed.

In conclusion the survey recommended:

1 Each country needs to improve its bibliographical control of microcopies either through a single national centre or a series of centres each with a different speciality. Centres should produce lists of projected and completed microcopying projects at least annually and and should liaise with each other internationally.

2 Production, storage and cataloguing should be standardised throughout the offices of the ISO (International Organisation for Standardisation), national standards organisations, IFLA (International Federation of Library Associations), FID (Federation International de Documentation) and the International Council on Archives. (Experience on standardisation suggests that a much shorter list would yield more rapid progress).

3 Production of an inventory of existing microcopies should precede programmes for future projects. Preparation of lists should begin at national level with details of foreign documents to be passed to the appropriate national centre.

4 Print outs are needed for documents in heavy use; improvements in both readers and reader-printers are needed.

5 The above recommendations will be sent out and consultations on implementation made by mail or by a symposium.

In 1968, three years after the publication of the recommendations, there is little obvious sign, with the notable exception of the U.S.A., of any implementation of the Unesco survey recommendations, although in Great Britain the question of legal deposit is being considered by the Copyright Committee of the Microfilm Association of Great Britain, while Dr. Van Der Wolk, of the Microfiche Foundation in the Netherlands, is known to have raised the matter at an international meeting of the foundation in late 1966.

The United States was already taking action at the time of the survey. Details of the American programme are given in a variety of sources (105 to 108, 116). The setting up of a National Register of Microform Masters was announced in October, 1964. The centre was to operate for its first two years under a $35,000 grant from the Council on Library Resources. The centre records the existence and location of master negatives of newspapers, serials and books, and makes the information available to other organisations. After the intitial two years the Register was to be produced as a supplement to the National Union Catalog. Items are arranged and identified by Library of Congress and National Union Catalog numbers (items without such numbers are listed separately). Two categories of master are included – *(a)* the master duplicating microform; *(b)* the master preservation microform which must be of archival quality stored in a suitable environment in a responsible non-profit making institution.

While the United States appears to be the only major country to have taken action in rationalising overall bibliographic control of published microforms, it has stopped short of legal deposit requirements. In Great Britain, what activity there has been has centred on the copyright committee of the Microfilm Association of Great Britain. In an unpublished report dated January 1968 (109) the committee draws attention to the fact that "There is much publication in microform of already published material. Preservation of this material is important because originals may be destroyed or in dangerously deteriorated condition". But the report concentrates on original microform publication. "In cases of original publication it is very important that the material should be conserved. Provision of legal deposit at the British Museum is just as imperative as for conventionally published material". In its recommendations the committee states that: "(1) Section 15 of the Copyright Act 1911 should be amended to include published works . . . whatever the means of manufacture of the copies . . . examples of published works are microtransparencies, microcards, magnetic tapes and, in the future, such forms as crystals".

However, the second recommendation stated that "only original publication should be covered in this way, except where, either because of date or place of publication, the original work was not subject to deposit". The remaining recommendations outline how the system should operate—the microform publisher should be legally obliged to offer a copy to the British Museum; the Museum, in exercising its option, should pay the cost of making a duplicate plus a handling charge. The British Museum should notify the British National Bibliography of publications offered to it as above.

The proposals, if adopted, would insure at least that microform copies of rare works not already in depository libraries would be assured of preservation (presumably, however, the micropublishers responsible for the original microrecording would want some assurance that the microcopy supplied as a legal deposit would not be used by the depository library for further duplication while the publisher's own negatives remained available for the purpose). Since they make no provision for works already subject to legal deposit which are micro-recorded, they would unfortunately not provide a good basis for a British equivalent to the American National Register of Microform Masters. Until such a register is produced, it will remain difficult to find out whether a given work or publication is available on microform from a British library and there will be the inevitable frustrations in searching and duplication in microrecording projects. Internationally the problem is greater; the United States with its National Register has provided a lead. A series of such registers from the major bibliographic powers would provide a very considerable contribution to the world of learning. France at least may be moving in this direction since it has established the Association Pour la Conservation et la Reproduction Photographique de la Presse (ACRPP). In its published Aims and Activities (289) the ACRPP states that it is creating a central file of French newspapers and periodicals on 35 mm roll from which it supplies microduplicates at a basic price per image of about 0.10 fr. For use with the file the ACRPP has developed a reader loaded by a form of cassette which takes reels holding 30-180 metres (90-540 feet—well above the standard 30 metre or 100 feet lengths). J. Prinet also describes (323) the activities of the ACRPP.

It must be remembered additionally that microcopy publishing is likely in the near future to evolve a new category of publications—in which already published material will be collected by specific subject or form, suitably organised and indexed, and the whole collection published as a "packaged" library for desk-top use. There are already proposals for this type of service from the Medical Research Council in its project "FAIR" (110) and from the National Reprographic Centre for documentation (111). So far as these services reissue already published material they are republishing; so far as they select and organise the material, they are producing original publications. Either way, common sense would indicate that such services are potentially valuable to the scholars of the future and also justify preservation at national level via a legal deposit system. (Original publication on microform is the subject of chapter five.)

In the United States the question of bibliographic identification of material excluded from the National Register is beginning to cause concern. H. J. Hilton (319) points out that there is no overall control or order in the identification systems used by major microfiche producers such as the Educational Resources Information Center, the Atomic Energy Commission and the Clearinghouse for Federal Scientific and Technical Information. He proposes a national system based on a two-part code number to overcome the problem. H. Wooster (329) suggests that the established CODEN number system should be used for report identification. The question of code identifications of this type is closely related to the operation of possible future copyright systems.

Cataloguing of microforms in libraries

W. Simonton, of the University of Minnesota Library School (112), reviews the bibliographic factors in the handling of microforms at individual library level. He states that traditionally librarians generally endeavour to provide a separate entry for each bibliographic independent work in the collection, but that no entries are provided for individual chapters. This system, Simonton considers, has established relative equilibrium between libraries' ability to acquire and their ability to catalogue. However, he notes that microforms may upset this equilibrium—it is possible to acquire at a single stroke 30,000 titles in Evans' "American Bibliography" at 25c per title but the cost of cataloguing each would be several times higher and probably prohibitive. (Similarly, in the scientific and technical field it is possible to acquire nearly 1,000 titles a year on microfiches of the Society of Automotive Engineers' technical papers). He goes on to suggest that realistically such collections should be treated as dependent rather than independent.

On the question of physical description in the catalogue, Simonton notes the existence of two theories: the facsimile theory and the edition theory. The former places emphasis on the original form and adds to this a description or statement of the microformat used—he considers this a convenient method, and the single description remains valid irrespective of media used for later reproduction. The edition theory emphasises the format of the moment and therefore requires a new description each time, wherever a new form of reproduction is employed. He notes that the Library of Congress now prefers the edition theory but in the past has employed the facsimile theory—he thinks it likely that the facsimile theory will be favoured in the revised cataloguing rules.

Simonton's prediction concerning the revised cataloguing rules has in fact proved broadly accurate since the new Anglo-American rules (290) apply the facsimile theory to all editions, the chief purpose of which is to provide replicas that reproduce as closely as possible the original. The rules also specify the form of entry for original micro-publications (i.e. publications which were issued on microforms in the first instance). These rules are in fact one of the few publications to utilise ISO terminology; microfiches are referred to as "Sheet" microfilm (microfiches).

T. P. Saxena and M. A. H. Saifuddin, of the Aligarh Muslim University Library, India (113), appear to favour the facsimile theory too, since they say that the entry should include a collation of the original together with that of the microform—details of the microform should state the number of reels or cards and also whether it is a positive or negative. But they raise several unanswered queries: which is the publishing date, that of the original or that of the copy? What happens if the microform is a collection of documents without covering title frames? If there are two or more works on one film, how are they to be described? If the material exists partly in original form and partly in microcopy, how should this be described? They recommend that a committee should be established to decide upon these questions.

Guidance on the form of descriptive entry relating to microcopies is forthcoming from R. B. Eckles (114). He considers that the form of entry used by the American Historical Association in its "Guide to photocopies of historical manuscripts in the United States and Canada" (115), is ideal and states that it has been adopted by the Library of Congress for the National Register of Microform Masters, the first issues of which are now available (116).

On the question of the shelf arrangement of microforms W. Simonton (112) sees six possibilities:

1 Arranging by the internal arrangement of microform series as published (sometimes, as on some micro-opaque cards, there is no option since more than one title may appear on the same card).

2 Strict accession or title order within each type of microform—said to be simple and efficient at least in space requirements.

3 Broad category arrangement by the form of the original (i.e. periodicals, books, newspapers, etc.)—said to be convenient and often corresponding to the users' approach.

4 A subject classification of the microform collection.

5 A broad subject classification with accession number or alphabetical sub-arrangements.

6 A complete classification of the microforms not merely on the shelf list but also on the shelves.

Retrospective micropublication: reprinting by microform

There are two distinct roles for microforms in the publishing fields. The traditional role embraces the use of microforms virtually as a reprinting or retrospective publishing medium; issues of journals or newspapers are published collectively, usually on roll film, when the end of a given year or volume has been reached, rare and out-of-print books, or manuscripts, are re-issued on microform. The newer role is that of a medium for original publication in which the microform is either the sole medium of publication or one which appears simultaneously as an optional alternative to the conventional publication. This section is concerned with the former more traditional application, which, so far as libraries are concerned, is frequently only a by-product of their recording for preservation programmes, while chapter five reviews original micro-publication.

The overall pattern presented by this area of application reveals a range of national and specialist libraries which generally play a relatively passive role by making available duplicate microcopies of material in their collections produced as a by-product of their preservation microcopying programmes, together with a number of commercial microform publishers more actively engaged in evaluating and anticipating the potential demand and making commercial decisions on the viability of given projects for micropublication purposes.

The libraries tend to play a passive role; if a negative microform has already been made for their stock, they will generally supply a positive copy subject to the requester making his own arrangements to obtain permission of the copyright owner, where applicable. Additionally, they will frequently micro-record material in their stock on behalf of a requester, subject again to the requester producing copyright clearance. This situation broadly applies, for example, to the University of London Library (75), to the Library of Congress (71), and certainly to the British Museum where an official (A. Desmond) has stated that the service is not widely known and "does not seek publicity" (165). It will be shown later in this survey that many authorities see libraries moving into a more active role in future systems. This is demonstrated by the recent announcement (291) that the New York Public Library is to make its entire microform stock of 25,000 reels available via the 3M company.

H. Lenneberg (349) outlines some of the problems encountered by American libraries in obtaining material on microfilm from European libraries. He suggests that the proportion of requests not met for one reason or another may be as high as one in three. In the discussion following Lenneberg's paper, it was suggested that the very age of some of the supplying libraries' buildings made the provision of adequate modern microrecording facilities difficult.

The commercial microform publishers tend to play a more active role; typically they may publish collections of material by subject or by form—for example theses and dissertations—or they may build up an extensive catalogue of books and periodicals available in microform; the coverage of the latter will normally be fairly random—some items will owe their inclusion to an original specific request, others (especially periodicals) to anticipation of a demand.

While the libraries have tended to produce only 35mm roll film (with the exception of some, mainly Dutch, libraries producing microfiches), the commercial publishers between them use a wide range of microforms—35mm roll, microfiches, ultrafiches, micro-opaque cards and most recently 16mm roll in cassettes.

The commercial microform publishers also publish in the accepted sense since they negotiate royalty arrangements with copyright owners where appropriate (but frequently material on which copyright has expired is involved). However, several publishers also copy on demand and add the work to their catalogue. For rare and out-of-print material commercial publishers rely mainly on library collections and usually maintain camera teams in or near the major libraries. Methods of recompense to the host libraries are financial or in kind (the supply of microcopies or reading equipment).

A. B. Veaner (292) noted in 1968 that micropublication was a major trend. He describes the "Microplate" shared preservation programme promoted jointly by the National Cash Register company and Rowman & Littlefield, in which disintegrating books would be recorded on PCMI; to qualify they must not exceed conventional size and possess a potential demand of 300 copies (Veaner comments that this figure would represent an attractive risk for a conventional reprint company).

He questions whether the confidence in the future of micropublication is not misplaced when the performance of so many micropublishers is poor. He states that every conceivable technical and bibliographic fault has been present in published microforms, with University Microfilms and the Microcard Corporation (now a subsidiary of the National Cash Register Company) the only notable exceptions.

Later in 1968 Veaner announced (346) a programme under the auspices of the American Library Association (ALA) to evaluate selected micropublications. He points out that, unlike conventional publications, micropublications are essentially invisible and it would be uneconomic for purchasers to evaluate and inspect each project. He lists eleven technical criteria, a similar number of administrative criteria and eight bibliographic criteria against which projects would be evaluated.

In December 1968 a report (347) appeared in the ALA's periodical 'Choice' on the first evaluation under the programme. This was an evaluation of the 'New York Times' on microfilm. The programme began in 1939 when University Microfilms were awarded the contract for current filming and the Recordak Division of Kodak the contract for filming the back files to 1851. This arrangement was maintained until 1967 during which period the technical quality was reported as satisfactory. In 1967 the 'New York Times' started to do its own microfilming and from this date the report notes a precipitous drop in quality. Faults included fogging, poor centring, bleed through of text from the other side of the page, inadequacies in resolution test target practice, in reproduction of half-tones and in processing scratching and incorrect spooling. The position, it states, is being rectified by re-filming,

The ALA's programme will clearly warrant the closest attention from micro-publishers and librarians. The absence of reviews of micro-publications was noted in the study carried out in 1964/65 by Unesco (see page 43). Perhaps the most useful outcome of the ALA's programme would be the appearance of reviews in a widening range of professional and commercial journals throughout the world. Where the limited size of the 'edition' precluded gifts of review copies in the accepted manner, the loan of review editions could be arranged in lieu—alternatively the reviews could be based on copies already purchased.

Some major commercial microform publishers and their programmes

1 Microcard Editions Inc.,
901 26th Street, NW,
Washington D.C. 20037, U.S.A.

Microcard Editions is a division of the Microcard Corporation which in 1967 became a subsidiary of the National Cash Register Company. Microcard Editions was established in the late 1940's to publish mainly on "Microcards" (a trade name registered in the United States denoting 5 x 3 inch micro-opaque cards). Where appropriate the company also publish on roll film. In 1963 (76) it was offering microfiches as an alternative to its "Microcards"—although somewhat reluctantly since it compared them unfavourably with micro-opaques, and prices for the microfiche versions were not listed and only available on application. By the following year (77), however, the company had experienced a change of heart—not only were prices quoted for the microfiche options but the unfavourable comparison had disappeared to be replaced by one in which they were shown to possess three advantages additional to those listed for micro-opaques. In addition to its publishing activities, the Microcard Corporation manufactures a step-and-repeat microfiche camera, microfiche readers, a micro-opaque reader (sold in Britain as the Recordak 6B) and a step-and-repeat enlarger/printer for microfiches. With the takeover by NCR it has become associated with the company responsible for the PCMI microfiche. Microcard equipment, with the exception noted above, is not sold in the United Kingdom.

The company provides an invaluable service to users in its annual cumulative publication "Guide to microforms in print" (78). This is a guide arranged alphabetically by author (journals, etc,. by title) to material in microtext available on a regular basis from United States Publishers. It excludes theses and dissertations. The current issue lists microform material from over 50 publishers and libraries. The use of the term 'in print' in the title of the guide represents a questionable extension of this printing term. Microforms are never 'in print' or 'out of print' in any real sense of the term once a master negative has been made. They are essentially a medium for duplication on demand with none of the questions of standing type, printing, collating and binding implicit in the conventional media. Entitled thus, the guide could be described as a list out-of-print in prints.

To cover its own publications the company issues annually the Microcard Microfiche catalog (79). Here the treatment is more detailed; it includes both alphabetical author and subject arrangements with entries in the author section fairly fully annotated. Each issue includes all the material currently available. No particular pattern of subject coverage emerges—chemistry is about the biggest ~~group~~ with thirty entries while British history, for instance, has about 15. Typically, most of the material is of the nineteenth or early twentieth century but the periodical "Encounter" 1953-61 is available and so are a microfiche or micro-opaque versions of the transcript of the trial of Adolph Eichmann by the Government of Israel.

2 Micromethods Ltd.,
East Ardsley, Wakefield, Yorks.
and
17 Denbigh Street, London, S.W.1.

Micromethods Ltd. is an indigenous British company and a subsidiary of Educational Productions Ltd. The basic function of Micromethods is micropublishing but they additionally carry out microfilm contract work and manufacture reading equipment (their range now includes only two models—the VC motor driven 35mm roll reader and the VC Executive microfiche and micro-opaque reader).

The company specialises in the publication on microforms of medieval manuscripts, rare and out-of-print books, university theses and local and other newspapers. It publishes on 35mm roll, microfiches or micro-opaques (it invariably offers an option on either of the latter at the same price but reports that a considerable shift in demand in favour of microfiches has taken place). The company issues irregularly a main catalogue (81) divided into broad fields by form or subject ("History", "Literature" and "Languages", "Technical and Science" and "Newspapers" are examples). The catalogue includes an uncertain percentage of material from other micro-publishers on behalf of whom Micromethods act as agents; it also includes full sized photocopies. The catalogue is particularly strong on British local newspapers, especially north country ones—presumably reflecting the Yorkshire location of the company. Micromethods are also the major publishers of microform copies of British university theses. Their catalogue of theses (82) includes over 1,000 theses arranged by identical subject heads to those in the Aslib Index to theses (83) and the Aslib reference number is quoted where possible. It is unfortunate that the catalogue has to carry the warning that print-outs are not recommended since many of the films have been prepared from carbon copies—the fact that good copies cannot be made available to a publisher suggests that universities may attach a low priority to the dissemination of information in theses.

3 The Readex Microprint Corporation,
New York N.Y., U.S.A.
address in Great Britain:
63 Great Russell Street,
London, W.C.1.

Readex are at present unique among microtext publishers in that their total activity is based on one type of microform—a 6 x 9 inch micro-opaque. Furthermore, the micro-opaque in this case is again unique in that it is not a photographic product but virtually a miniature offset print. There is no precise published information available on the production method used. Each Microprint card holds up to one hundred images in ten rows of ten and contains an eye legible title. Collections of the cards are supplied in labelled boxes which the publishers suggest can be interfiled with ordinary book stock.

Readex began publishing in 1960 and now claim nearly 1 million titles. The publishing programme concentrates on American and British government research materials. Hansard's parliamentary debates, the Journal of the House of Commons and the House of Commons sessional papers are typical productions. A range of current and historical government publications are also offered. The Readex Microprint Catalogue (84) is well produced, annotated at length and illustrated. It contains an alphabetical index. Readex are thought to be working on the development of an offset printing process for transparencies—

thus producing a Microprint microfiche. They also sell a cheap micro-opaque/microfiche reader—the Readex model D. (The Micromethods VC executive is the only other reader on the British market able to handle Readex Microprint cards.)

4 Research Publications NV,
Leiden, Holland
address in Great Britain:
Inter Documentation Co. (U.K.) Ltd.,
c/o India Office Library,
Orbit House, 197 Blackfriars Road,
London, S.E.1.

Research Publications is a sister company to both the Inter Documentation Co. AG and the International Documentation Centre AB—the reason for these titular variations is said to lie in the complexities of company registration in the various countries. The Research Publications group produce solely on microfiches—originally in the popular continental size 90 x 120mm, latterly on international A6 size. It is instructive to examine their method of working (85):

1 Various specialised fields of knowledge are decided upon on the recommendation of advisory committees and experts in the field.

2 A bibliography of material is compiled, normally on the basis of (a) significance to the field; (b) rarity or difficulty of access.

3 Research Publications then set about tracing the material and make appropriate arrangements to record it using one of their local camera units (which operate from Helsinki, Stockholm, Leiden and London).

4 The bibliography of material about to become available is published—it includes references to full sized reprints and microforms available from other sources.

Approximately 17 bibliographies have already been made available in this way including the following subjects: botany, zoology, geology, Africa, Near East, South Asia, Central Asia, East Asia and Slavonics.

It is reported (85) that over 90% of Research Publications' output goes to the United States; very little is sold in Europe and British sales are particularly low—reflecting probably the ready availability of rare materials in these areas. L. H. Hattery reports (171) that the International Documentation Centre sold 2½ million microfiches in 1965.

5 University Microfilms Inc.,
313 North 1st Street,
Ann Arbor, Mich., U.S.A.

address in Great Britain:
University Microfilms Ltd.,
St. John's Road, Tylers Green,
Penn, Bucks.

University Microfilms Inc. is a subsidiary of the Xerox Corporation; its British subsidiary, University Microfilms Ltd., was at one time a subsidiary of Rank Xerox Ltd., but has subsequently reverted to being under the direct control of the Xerox Corporation and University Microfilms Inc.

It is reported (86) that University Microfilms has three basic areas of activity:

1 The republishing of newspapers and periodicals on 35mm roll.

2 The reprinting of out-of-print books via 35mm roll and Xerox "Copyflo" electrostatic print-out.

3 Edition reprinting of books via offset—this does not involve a microfilm stage and is generally used where the known demand is in excess of 100 copies.

The University Microfilm periodicals' catalogue (87) includes over 1,700 titles. The entries are designated either as current or backfiles; items designated as current are only supplied where the purchaser affirms that the normal paper edition is also subscribed to (a constraint that is presumably written into contracts by the original publishers). The price system is based on a charge of 1/3c per page irrespective of demand. Reduction ratio employed is generally 1:17.

The University Microfilm catalogue of out-of-print books now includes 12,000 titles although, in fact, it has been built up purely in response to demands for specific items—no speculative micro-recording is done.

A major feature of the company's activities in the U.S.A. consists of the publishing of dissertations. The new DATRIX service provides facilities for computerised searches on dissertation material available.

Other major commercial firms issuing microtext catalogues include: The Lost Cause Press of Louisville, Kentucky; Micro Photo, of Cleveland, Illinois; a division of Bell & Howell, The Princeton Microfilm Corporation, Box 235, Princeton JCT NJ 08550, U.S.A. (16mm negative roll); and The Atlantic Microfilm Corporation, Spring Valley, New York 10977, U.S.A. (optional 16mm roll or microfiches). Altogether Microcard's 'Guide to Microforms in Print' lists 54 micropublishers.

The National Register of Microform Masters

The major non-commercial source of information on publications on microforms is the Library of Congress National Register of Microform

Masters (116). The overall bibliographic significance of the National Register has been reviewed elsewhere. The first issue of the register appeared in September, 1965. It included books (American and foreign), serials, pamphlets, newspapers and non-American dissertations. It excludes technical reports, typescript translations, archival manuscript collections, and U.S. doctoral dissertations and masters' theses. In the broad area covered, the National Register is clearly destined to become a source of information of international significance.

Previous to the publication of the National Register, the ground is less well covered. A major source of information is the "Union list of Microfilms" (143); this first appeared from the Philadelphia Bibliographic Center and Union Library Catalogue in 1942. Then, according to A. Diaz (142), it went through an involved series of accumulations and supplements until 1961, when a final accumulation was published by Edwards Brothers. An important restraint on the use of the list is that it is restricted to roll films only.

Unfortunately, between this date and the first issue of the National Register for Microform Masters in September, 1965, there is (again according to A. Diaz) an unsatisfactory interim period in which coverage was only maintained by the Library of Congress Microfilm Clearinghouse Bulletin, issued as an appendix to the Library of Congress Information Bulletin.

Newspapers, however, remained adequately covered throughout the period following the appearance of "Newspapers on Microfilm"(144) which ran through a succession of editions during which the responsibility for its publication was taken over by the Library of Congress. Since newspapers are being included in the National Register of Microform Masters, it may be uncertain whether this more specialised list will continue independently.

Other Union Lists

There are two particularly useful catalogues available; one from a commercial publisher—The Scarecrow Press—and the other a specialist subject list on the social sciences from the Maison des Sciences de l'Homme.

The first (88) a "Union list of publications in opaque microforms", compiled by Eva Tilton, is a 744-page publication now in its second edition. The compiler explains in a foreword that entries are, with few exceptions, those given by publishers and that the main arrangement is a list oriented to keyword rather than exact catalogue entries. In fact the main arrangement is predominantly by author but occasionally the subject or biography intrudes in lieu of the author. A comprehensive index at the back to subject, series and authors (that is those not included in heads in the main arrangement) makes the list easy and reliable to use, provided that the need for reference to both main arrangement and index is realised. The work of 26 publishers is included—all of American origin with the exception of Micromethods Ltd. and the International Documentation Centre AB. Entries total 7,640; each is serially numbered with the serial number functioning as the address for indexing purposes.

This list is a very useful contribution but ultimately the relevance of a single microform medium as a basis for a union list is questionable—especially in this case, since a high proportion of the opaque material listed would also be available on microfiches.

The Maison des Sciences de l'Homme issued its two-volume list of reviews and series (89) published in microform in September, 1965. The list is arranged in a simple alphabetical title order. It lists material from 26 micro-publishers—any hopes that the list would reveal substantial, otherwise unknown micro-publishing activities in the French speaking world are largely disappointing since only one of the publishers listed (L'Association pour la Conservation et le Reproduction Photographique de la Presse) is French and only a further four are European, the remainder consisting of ubiquitous American publishers. Prices quoted are those of the country of origin. The list embraces the following specific subjects in the social sciences field: philosophy and religion, anthropology, ethnography, pure history, folklore, linguistics and philology, psychology, teaching and education, sociology, political science, economics, statistics, demography, geography, history, archaeology, fine arts but not literature. There is no subject index but this represents a most useful publication, more especially if it is to be regularly updated.

The proceedings of the symposium on microtexts as media for publication (90), held at Hatfield College of Technology in 1959, contain extensive lists of various types of microform publishers. In his contribution to the seminar, Dr. L. J. Van der Wolk lists eleven microfiche publishers—eight from the Netherlands, one French, one British, one Polish. Appendix 2 of the proceedings lists 41 microform publishers, including some of those listed by Van der Wolk. These lists are particularly useful—especially that of Dr. Van der Wolk—since they include some relatively unknown sources.

Although it is not strictly relevant to microtext publishing as such, the use of microform as an intermediate for producing enlarged books for partially sighted users should not be overlooked. In a press release (99) in March, 1966, University Microfilms Ltd. announced a new service offered by the National Library of the Blind, 35 Great Smith Street, London S.W.1. The books are microrecorded and printed out at approximately twice their original size on Rank Xerox "Copyflo" equipment.

Microtext reading room design

The question of microtext reading rooms is an interesting one; the microtext reading room is purely a library phenomenon—in no other field of microform application—engineering drawings and business records for example—has it apparently been found necessary to allocate specific rooms for microform reading purposes. The first matter for examination therefore is that of the necessity for such a room; clearly they were thought necessary in the past in libraries—do they remain necessary? No author appears to have specifically raised this question.

The reasons for the need for rooms in the past are not difficult to arrive at:

1 Due to the inadequacies of back projector readers with translucent screens, front projectors with opaque screens have been found more satisfactory for the continuous reading requirements in libraries. Front projection implies an external optical path and from this comes the problem of the impingement of ambient light on the screen resulting in loss of contrast leading to the need for a darkened area. The influence of this factor appears to be diminishing due to:

(a) Translucent screen materials have improved and are becoming closer to opaque screens in performance although mostly they still have a considerable way to go before anything akin to equality is attained.

(b) More powerful light sources (quartz halogen) for external projection systems are being used, making for a greater tolerance of ambient light especially in shielded screen designs.

2 Noise from motor-driven roll film readers was a problem and is still likely to remain so in study areas of libraries but much could be done by specifying quiet running motors; acoustic booths might also be effective. An increasing percentage of readers will be microfiche readers—virtually silent in operation.

3 Microforms and associated equipment have been regarded as delicate as to both environment and handling. In fact, as British Standard 1153 (118) makes clear, the requirements for the storage of working as opposed to preservation film are very moderate. "The temperature need not be maintained within close limits. The temperature suitable for habitable rooms would be satisfactory. Relative humidity should be kept below 60% if possible." The requirements for microforms needed for preservation are more critical but even these are similar to those needed in any case for the preservation of paper. The equipment and handling problems necessitating the level of control possible in a separate room are associated mainly with roll film readers and are due entirely to the absence of cassette loading equipment in library systems. (Several

authorities, Dickison in (62) and Williams and Wright in (68), have already drawn attention to the problems created by reel-loading systems).

There can be little doubt that the relegation of users to work in separate rooms in semi-darkness has scarcely encouraged the exploitation of microforms.

In view of the likely increase in the use of microforms in libraries, it seems most likely that reading rooms will give way to reading stations consisting of groups of readers situated at various points throughout libraries.

D. C. Weber (117) gives design criteria for reading rooms. He assumes the problem to be one of reading room design in a new building. The first decision is said to be whether to centralise or de-centralise the reading room facilities. A centralised facility gives economy in operation, efficiency in library organisation, protection of materials, efficient equipment utilisation. A decentralised facility gives greater user convenience and groups all material together by subject. He is also in favour of centralisation on the need for air conditioning and the delicacy of equipment. As to location, he considers the room should be near the main reference collection and also near to the cataloguing department since cataloguing staff need access to readers when handling microforms. He points out that the microform store is likely to grow faster than the main collection. He lays some emphasis on the value of one person being responsible for the administration of the room. The desk space should be sufficient to accommodate a reader and space for note-taking or a typewriter together with book space for material to be used in conjunction with the microtext; the minimum desk area on this basis should be 2 x 4 feet, far better 3 x 5 feet with a total of 40 square feet for each reading station. He distinguishes between working film in the reading room and master film in air conditioned vaults. Sheet film should be stored in drawers of the appropriate size; roll film in cabinets 42-48 inches high or on book shelves. Acoustic control is necessary because of machine noise and a staff operating manual should be drawn up detailing maintenance and similar matters.

C. F. Scott (119) describes the reading room of the University of London. The floor area is said to be 600 square feet and the room has 10 reading stations, main table sizes are 4-6 inches x 2 foot, and additionally there are 6 smaller 2 x 2 foot tables.

Scott notes that the rectangular tables have proved too narrow for some reader models (thus confirming the desirability of dimensions suggested by Weber); the general lighting is reduced to a minimum using window blinds. Scott relates that most users bring their own microforms (not surprisingly in view of the fact that he describes library policv as that of buying microforms only where no alternative existed).

He states that use has been 20-30 per cent of capacity and that the growth of the collection has been slowed down as a result of the development of electrostatic full sized copying; contrary to Weber's theories he believes that use of the reading rooms will continue to slow down under the added influence of improved print-out devices. He points out that arts libraries are less affected by microforms and questions whether the room should have been made as large as it is. The library is said to have no pressing space problem (but at the price of locating part of its stock in a remote store).

Quality control, administration and standards in libraries

Quality control in library micro-recording departments has much in common with general quality control in other areas of application. However, together with retrospective publishing, it poses in many ways the most stringent requirements; in both the engineering drawing field (because of the need for production print-out) and in original publishing (because of the multi-generation aspect of microtext publishing) there is a need for high standard of quality. However, active engineering systems are by definition handling new drawings produced to a standard suitable for micro-recording* while original publishing on microform also presupposes new originals—and the ability again to produce originals specifically suited to micro-recording (i.e. of good line-to-background contrast and the avoiding of fine detail in text or diagrams) is frequently implicit in the system.

Only in micro-recording for library purposes and for retrospective publishing is one confronted on the one hand by fine detail in text or illustration on paper that has become degraded by age or wear and tear, and on the other by requirements to produce microforms suitable for continuous reading after multi-generation reproduction.

A. B. Veaner, writing in 1963 (120), noted that there is a complete absence of a guide to quality control for producers of library microforms. He considers that the library field demands specialised techniques due to the wide variety of originals that need to be filmed. He goes on to suggest simple techniques that may overcome some problems: show-through from a preceding page can be overcome by the insertion of a black backing sheet; if recorded from the other side of the page it can be eliminated by means of a white opaque sheet (the effect is to increase the contrast of the original).

He suggests the areas that a shop manual should cover: (a) Bookholders (most of which he considers are suitable only for easy-to-handle books; the "Graflex" is useless for small books while the "Photostate" is unsuitable for production work) – the shop manual

* *A British standard (271) for this purpose was published in 1967.*

should review the state-of-the-art in bookholders. (b) Orientation of the camera head for both normal figuration (left to right) and oriental (right to left). (c) Choice of, and buying of, equipment. (d) Film selection of exposure, minimising film consumption, adjustment of camera lights, use of resolution targets, standardised reductions, application of serial numbers to frames, bench layouts for film inspection, footage and density measurements, spooling, boxing and marking – additionally, a handbook on processing was badly needed.

Finally, he suggests a specific list of contents for a manual:

1 Definitions of purpose stating the various functions of microreproduction clearly.
2 List of standards.
3 Terminology.
4 Policy decisions for reproduction services.
5 Administration.
6 Specific techniques.
7 Ordering of microfilm copies.
8 Maintaining and servicing microtext materials.
9 Use of hand cameras.
10 Summary of copyright.
11 Classified bibliography.
12 Brief history.

In 1964 something akin to Veaner's concepts of a shop manual appeared with the publication of Specifications for Library of Congress microfilming by S. R. Salmon (121). The manual deals with the subject under five headings:

1 *Preparation.* The file or book is to be checked for completeness, any missing parts have to be obtained, out of order pages re-arranged, creases and wrinkles to be removed with an electric iron or in a press.

2 *Filming.* Material requiring more than one roll should be divided on a bibliographically acceptable basis. Targets:—each reel to commence and end with "start" and "end" targets; a target giving standard bibliographical data should follow the "start" target and precede the "end" target (size of target lettering is specified, image placement to accord with ASA PH5.3–1958 (292)*; reduction ratios ranging between 14 and 30 are specified for various sizes of original; film stock to be in accordance with ASA PH1.25 (294) and for permanent preservation with ASA PH1.28 (123); resolution to be at least 125 lines per millimetre, unperforated film to be used; background density to lie between 1.2 and 1.5.

* *British equivalent would be BS 1371 (125).*

3 *Inspection.* Films to be checked as quickly as possible after processing; density readings to be taken every few feet; faulty frames to be retaken and spliced by using a heat-welded splice.

4 *Positive Copies.* Resolution to be at least 100 lines per millimetre.

5 *Storage.* In accordance with ASA PH5.4 (124)*. Reels should comply with ASA PH5.6 (295) (the appropriate British Standard would be BS 1371 (125)).

D. C. Holmes also provides a general article on quality control at the Library of Congress in (126).

J. W. Boone (328) analysed the administrative practices in library photographic services by means of a questionnaire sent to 45 libraries in the U.S.A. Data was obtained on equipment, organisation, personnel and financial policies. Not surprisingly the author notes wide deviations in practice.

Standards

That the distinction between shop manuals and standards is a fine one is demonstrated by the most significant general code of practice published, relating to library microforms, "Microfilm Norms", published in 1967 by the American Library Association (127). "Microfilm Norms" is concerned primarily with the production and use of complete books on 35mm roll film intended for permanent preservation libraries. As in the Library of Congress Specifications, it is based wherever possible on published American Standards. "Microfilm Norms" contains a list of standards with which it is to be used in conjunction, definitions, target descriptions (it specified; the use of a hypo test patch for assessment of archival quality, an identification target, a technical target for resolution testing and scaling, a bibliographic target to ensure consistency in description with that of the original). Target arrangement, reduction ratios (to be 14x except for material too large which has to be done at 20x), sectional filming and other matters are also specified. Resolution for negatives is set at 5.6 pattern of the NBS test chart (and therefore at the standard 14x reduction calls only for a modest 78.4 lines per millimetre; even at the alternative 20x it is only 112 lines per millimetre, somewhat low in relation to other standards), while resolution for second generation positives is set at an appropriately lower figure.

The question of standardisation of microforms in libraries has already been touched on in the review of the failures in previous library microtext systems in which it was noted that authorities such as R. R. Dickison (62) and W. R. Hawken (68) and Unesco (131) considered the lack of it was restraining the use of microforms in libraries. Hawken, (68) in dealing with 35mm roll (the traditional medium for libraries), criticises not so much the lack of standards but the basis upon which they are conceived. He queries the system which encourages extreme flexibility as to frame size and orientation at the production stage, leading to a similar requirement for extremely flexible and therefore expensive reading devices. On this basis he considers that: "In over 30 years of use very little has been done to establish useful standards for the production of 35mm roll film", and he notes that, while "Microfilm Norms" (127) and "Specifications for Library of Congress Microfilming" (121) make recommendations on document sizes vis-a-vis reduction ratios, no recommendations are made as to image size, and therefore neither offer any real hope for resolving the long standing problem of low cost user equipment such as readers and reader-printers.

Hawken's points certainly are worthy of close examination by standards committees. Experience in practice has to be accumulated before standards can be written but there is a danger that the establishment of the practice, and more particularly the interests of equipment manufacturers on which the practices are based, tend to influence the resultant standards to an excessive degree. Additionally, the standards which Hawken criticises may well have been appropriate when 35mm roll was a relatively inactive medium used in a small number of libraries—a situation in which the price of the low number of reader units required would be scarcely a major issue. It may well be that as 35mm roll moves into more active use in a wider range of libraries (or conversely, if it is to do so), some tightening in the production standards leading towards cheaper and more standardised user equipment should be considered.

In view of Hawken's comments and the general question, raised above, of tightening the range of options in 35mm recording, it is fair to note that "Microfilm Norms" (127) does at least restrict reduction ratios for precisely these reasons: "In order to simplify the design of new equipment and to facilitate microfilm re-enlargement to paper copy, the standard reduction has been set at 14x, and for originals too large to be accommodated at this reduction at 20x". This is in contrast to some earlier generation standards exemplified in BS 1371 (125) which has nothing at all to say about reduction ratios. It is particularly disappointing to note, however, that the draft ISO standard on 16 and 35mm microrecording also refrains from making recommendations on reduction ratios. It must be remembered that, as borne out both by Hawken in (68) and the National Bureau of Standards study (below) (129), recommendations on reduction ratios related to document sizes (external formats) need qualifying by relating them additionally to type sizes or fitness of detail (internal format) and to overall condition of the original (poor condition originals may present a low contrast between text and background) if legibility on microforms is to be assured.

The problems created in considering overall standards for libraries are brought out by a study carried out by the U.S. National Bureau of Standards into the requirements and specifications for serial and monograph recording at the National Library of Medicine (129). The study was carried out by the NBS because the National Library of Medicine found itself confronted by the problem of a large stock of valuable printed material which was gradually deteriorating. The NBS team carried out a detailed study in depth of the characteristics of the material involved, and the results were correlated against the presently available performance of micro-photographic materials and recording systems. A very high basic performance standard was set: that the optimum reduction ratio for recording the collection "is the highest reduction that will routinely achieve the visual legibility requirement of eight lines per millimetre when an enlargement is made from the third generation microform". (The normal human eye is considered to be capable of resolving up to 10 line pairs per millimetre. There would be no point therefore in presenting an eye-legible image exceeding this figure but 8 line pairs per millimetre represents a resolution probably twice as high as that which the user is normally likely to find on enlargement from a third generation microform. It does not guarantee legibility, since this can only be a function of the legibility of the original which itself may be on or beyond the borderline of legibility, but it does ensure that the finest detail visible to the unaided eye on the original could be visible on a microform magnified or printed out to a similar size.)

After the detailed analysis of document characteristics against this criterion, the NBS team recommended that the maximum reduction should be no higher than 12x.

This figure is enormously significant—it is below the minimum of 14x in "Microfilm Norms" and similar specifications, it effectively eliminates all microforms using a 16mm frame size (16mm roll and the microfiche, both of which normally involve reductions in excess of 18x), and leaves the 35mm frame as the smallest option.

The report then goes on to suggest that reduction optical printing can be used to print down the more popular (and presumably, therefore, more legible) items on to 16mm roll or microfiche at cumulative reductions of less than 24x. If demand is sufficient, the possibility of cumulative reductions up to 240x (presumably with a view to dissemination on PCMI or Microvue microfiches) are envisaged.

Universal adoption of the basic standard of 8 lines per millimetre from an enlargement made from a third generation microform established by the NBS team would constitute a major step in establishing microforms as a medium suitable for continuous reading. On this basis the reports merit the most serious attention.

In addition to commenting on 35mm roll film, W. R. Hawken (68) also examined the basis of the COSATI microfiche Standard (64) upon which the British Standard 4187 (5) for microfiches has been based. These do possess the fixed frame size and restricted range of reduction ratios permitting the use of simple low cost readers but Hawken queries whether the frame sizes are not too small and the reductions (18x plus) too high for library materials. He points out that the COSATI standard was written around the requirements of U.S. Government reports produced in typescript, and not around the fine detail and small character sizes found in printed originals. He draws support for these arguments from the study made for the National Library of Medicine (129) and particularly its recommendation that reduction ratios should not exceed 1:12.

Additionally Hawken reports on the results of a study that he had carried out, sponsored by the Library Technology Program of the American Library Association. In this he found that even with 12 point type—a fairly generous size, larger than those frequently used in scientific publishing—stroke and space widths of as little as 0.2mm and 0.1mm were not uncommon (the NLM study had found that journals frequently used characters 1.0 to 1.2mm high with some important information characters below 1mm). Hawken considered his findings corroborated those of the National Library of Medicine study.

These two items are worthy of the closest consideration by standards committees; the great bulk of microrecording for publishing and library purposes is now onto 16mm frame sizes with reduction ratios of 18:1 to 22:1. What is the significance quantatively of material with physical characteristics which make it unsuited to recording onto 16mm frames at these ratios? How, in terms of standards, can such documents be identified and subsequently how catered for? The question of returning to the use of full 35mm frames would demand the most careful consideration and ultimately the co-operation of manufacturers in producing modern readers for the purpose. Existing 35mm roll film readers for the library field are of archaic design. Roll film adaptations of 35mm aperture card readers produced for the engineering drawing market are generally unsatisfactory since the screens with the longest dimensions in the horizontal are unsuitably oriented for library material; additionally the facility for rotating the image is seldom present.

That technology may be on the point of providing an alternative solution to these dilemmas is suggested by the content of papers by S. B. Gray (315) and S. R. Ray (316). Gray describes how computer controlled cathode ray tube scanners may be used to obtain good quality microfilm images from poor quality originals of engineering drawings. The technique involves a class of density decision functions which assign a black/white bit decision to each density point and on the basis of this chooses that threshold which best preserves line and character detail. In practice the aperture card with a sub-standard image is placed in the scanner, an optimum binary picture is stored digitally, then an unexposed film is placed in the same scanner which then 'writes' the enhanced image onto it. The greatest problem is said to be in 'software'—each program is highly complex. Techniques of this type are collectively referred to as image enhancement techniques.

Ray discusses an ultra microfiche based dissemination and retrieval system and suggests that small print originals with details too fine for incorporation directly into the system should be automatically re-formatted. He suggests that a microfiche copy of the original should be subject to automatic analysis and the results would be fed to a second microfiche camera which records selected areas at a controlled magnification; normally one text page image would not be defected into more than two reformatted images. He suggests that the method would be quicker and easier than one based on character recognition.

Bibliographic presentation

In all this there remains a further significant gap—there are few available standards setting out the requirements for bibliographic procedures in micro-recording. 35mm roll is catered for by "Microfilm Norms" (127) but no British or international standards as yet exist (no American standards strictly of official national status exist either, but this situation will presumably change as the activities of the newly formed United States of America Standards Institute (264) get underway).

"Microfilm Norms" (127) specifies the type sequence and format and placement of bibliographic and other targets on 35mm roll, and measures to be taken over illegible, mutilated or missing or incorrectly paginated pages, and the lengths of leaders and trailers. The most significant strictly bibliographic requirements call for: (a) the provision at the beginning and end of the film proper of an identification target (that is an eye legible caption accompanied by "start" or "finish" as appropriate); (b) a technical target containing an NBS resolution chart and a scale measure from which reduction/magnification can be deducted; (c) a supplementary target to be used if the higher of the two permitted reduction ratios is used in any part of the film; (d) a bibliographic target—a form designed to ensure that the microcopy re-issue receives the same bibliographic description as the original and (e) a supplementary bibliographic target to be used where the original occupies more than one reel, in which case the supplementary target describes the specific contents of the reel in question and its number.

Bibliographic presentation and arrangement on microfiches remains as yet uncatered for in national standards, but a standard (128) has been produced by the Warren Spring Laboratory of the Ministry of Technology. It is based on the requirements of periodical recording on microfiche and lays down a basis for the way in which individual articles should be recorded and the unnecessary avoidance of dividing them between microfiche. It specifies the use of the CODEN reference in addition to normal periodical title and cites British Standard 4187 (5) on technical requirements.

Williams, in (59), also suggests that publishers should indicate the location of material on microfiches in terms of column and row co-ordinates rather than page numbers. Where appropriate, column and row co-ordinates could be added to page number locations in contents lists.

Future microform applications in libraries

The future role of microforms in library systems is seen by many authorities to lie in (a) much wider exploitation as a low cost dissemination media replacing to varying degrees established loan or circulation systems; (b) the use of microform stores permitting rapid and sometimes automated access to material by address codes supplied during separate subject search operations on indexes or via computers.

L. B. Heilprin, of the Council on Library Resources (U.S.A.), has produced two papers on the changing role of libraries as communicators of information; in the first (139) he examines the fundamentals of the communication process. He states that communication engineering is divided into two parts: the first, short duration (SD) messages lasting from a fraction of a micro-second to a few minutes; the second, long duration (LD) messages lasting from a few minutes to many centuries. Until recently, the term "communication engineer" had been used only for engineers of SD messages; engineers of LD messages had not been recognised as communications engineers but had been known as publishers, librarians, film manufacturers, manufacturers of copying equipment, optical designers and the like. Communications of both types are concerned with the propagation of "messages". All messages consist of two parts; a physical medium or body to carry the message and "modulation" which transforms the carrier into a modulated carrier of "message". SD messages can be transmitted by solid, liquid or gaseous states (for example, smoke rings or sounds—both of which soon die away), LD messages are confined to solids which may be modulated by a variety of techniques (writing, printing, engraving and the like). A fundamental difference between the two types is that SD messages are not archival since they require energy renewal to remain in existence; LD messages on solids do not, and are therefore relatively permanent.

Both types of message must be transmitted as efficiently as possible (the biological necessity for survival based on competition). Efficiency in SD messages consists in transmitting the maximum amount of information in the least time for the lowest costs; the general objective for LD messages is similar but in this case the modulation is not temporal but spatial—files per unit volume per dollar are a possible criterion. Efficiency in LD messages has tended to concentrate on reducing the volume of the solid carrier—LD carriers have long been effectively two dimensional with the third dimension reduced to a very thin layer (e.g. paper). Microforms fit into the picture by striving for improved efficiency in LD messages by compressing the modulation into a smaller space per unit of information (more file per square inch), and this is achieved by reduction. He goes on to note that reduction ratios as high as 1,000:1 have been attained. This permits recording of the Bible on $\frac{1}{4}$ of a square centimetre or 25 Bibles per square inch, while even this has been exceeded by Goldberg who achieved 50 Bibles per square inch (since Heilprin's paper National Cash Register have published the Bible on 2 square inches at 200:1). A 6 point type at normal viewing distance requires a resolution of 4 lines per millimetre; at 1,000 reduction 4,000 lines per millimetre are therefore required to restore 4 lines per millimetre to an original scale copy. McCamy is stated by Heilprin to have estimated the limit for reduction to this standard as 500-600 diameters. As the volume is reduced, the size of the carrier practical for human handling cannot correspondingly be reduced—accordingly it becomes necessary to store a large number of images together. (The alternative is to mount the microform into a larger carrier as in the aperture card). Heilprin states that in 1959 he roughly estimated the optimum reduction for libraries, taking into account space savings in libraries and the cost of microform equipment, at 25:1. Heilprin considers duplicating libraries to be the most significant development in view of the gradually falling costs of duplicating information.

In a second paper (67) he sees libraries as one of the stages in the communication path between authors and recipients of information. He sees the communication flow as proceeding from (1) the author, through (2) the publisher and (3) the library to (4) the user, but he notes that in a circulating or "C" library the flow line has a loop in it in that such libraries provide LD messages as output to the user but require them to be returned as part of the lending or circulating system. This non unidirectional flow always involves a power loss—based on CLR information, he states that this "power loss" (the cost of the loans system) accounts for 10% of the operating costs of large research libraries and 80% of that of small circulating libraries. For the circulation loop to disappear, Heilprin deduces that it is necessary to show that the cost of the item circulated is below that of the cost of the circulation routines—at that point it becomes cheaper to give away rather than loan. This situation he considers has already been reached. Firstly by paperbacks (which need to be returned on average only once in many cases to justify giving up circulation control) and, of more importance, by two other factors: LD messages used by scientists for communication have tended to become shorter (nearly all modern discoveries are announced in short articles or letters rather than books), while at the same time costs of propagating the messages by copying have decreased. Heilprin notes that many libraries already function as "D" (i.e. duplicating) libraries to a large extent, in that they photocopy rather than loan. He goes on to say that it is easy to see that, if dissemination was wholly by copying, libraries could optimise their economic costs, originals would be stored as masters for further duplication, and significantly the "D" library would be financially more independent than the "C" library, since it can charge the cost of copying to individual users. Future authors might derive a large fraction of their income from a revised copyright system in which clearing houses redistributed royalties based on records of copies made. Heilprin then develops an economic model of a "D" library tending to prove its viability. At the same time he notes the emergence of the "D" library at the Library of Congress, The Defense Documentation Center, The U.S. Patent Office, the New York Public Library, etc. Complete operating "D" libraries are demonstrated by the U.S. Air Force's Kodak "Minicard" system, the Central Intelligence Agency's IBM "Walnut" system, and potential systems are demonstrated, among others listed, by the National Cash Register's PCMI system.

P. Scott, of Massachusetts Institute of Technology, writing (140) of the contribution of microrecording to MIT's Project Intrex, sees a number of advantages in microphotography:

1 The attribute of combining, in a simple manner, alpha numeric as well as pictorial and other graphic information.

2 The full document can be handled mechanically—the single most important property of the technique.

3 Automatic, rapid access to any document or a section of any document is technically simple.

4 There are many different forms, each of which can be readily modified to meet the demands of particular applications.

5 Microforms lend themselves well to the demands of the non-circulatory library since output can take many forms—screen image, micro-image, duplicate, temporary intermediate plates, and full-sized paper copy.

6 The collection can remain complete at all times.

7 Microforms as a method of publication achieve remarkable economy irrespective of edition size (which need not even be predetermined).

8 Storage space is reduced giving lower building and building maintenance costs each year.

9 Space reduction and inherent publication economy reduce the need for transmitting information from one locale to another—this is valuable in view of the technical difficulties and costs of such transmission.

10 On the other hand, when transmission is necessary, the machine handled film is easier to control than a book.

11 Technically, the generation of full-sized paper copies is easier and subsequently more economical than from paper originals.

He notes that microforms are making considerable headway in industrial applications, and he considers that they could be of great value in the library, provided that systems are furnished and just not components. He considers that most of the earlier microforms applications in libraries failed to grow due to lack of systems design, and therefore do not provide a good basis for evaluation. In suggesting experiments for Project Intrex, he proposes the main objective to be the design and field trial of total systems. Components to be standardised for the greatest number of applications, but user satisfaction should not be compromised in the process. Specific questions need answering: What is the best manner in which computer inter-action with a microforms system can be achieved? What are the types of information that benefit from systems combining documents with descriptions in machine-readable form? Should the descriptors use magnetic striping or photo-digital form? Are very high reduction ratios worthwhile? An attempt should be made to perfect an intermediate step between the hard copy and the soft screen image—this could be a re-usable plate on which the full-sized image could be comfortably read and the plate subsequently returned to the machine for erasure and re-use. New materials should be tested in working systems. Slower films like diazo and Kalvar, at present used only for duplicating, have an advantage in being capable of handling in normal room lighting and therefore the potential for allowing instant micro-recording. (Since Scott's paper Caps Equipment have produced a prototype Kalvar camera.) Since film speed is relative to available optics and light sources, experiments should be put in hand—lasers as a light source might be worth investigating. There is a need for better trained technicians, and a course in the theory and practice of microphotography would be worthwhile.

Scott finally provides a list of considerations for microform systems design:

(a) An analysis of the character of input information, sizes, graphic aspects, storage arrangements (random or sequential?), growth rate, initial volume.

(b) User requirements—to be consulted simultaneously by 10, 100 or 1,000 people. Is remote consultation needed? What type of output forms?

(c) Which microform is best suited to the type of information and user requirements?

(d) What standards are needed?

(e) Which photographic materials are suited—silver, diazo, Kalvar, or all three?

(f) What are the economic constraints?

(g) How to attain compatibility of the micro-store with

(i) the rest of the library,

(ii) with other mechanised systems in the library?

(h) What type and amount of information should be in machine readable form on the microform—should it be a simple address in digital form or a series of machine readable descriptors?

(i) What should the reduction ratio be?

A detailed review of the current status of graphic storage techniques and their potential application to library mechanisation was presented by S. N. Alexander and F. C. Rose of the National Bureau of Standards to the Conference on libraries and automation at the Airlie Foundation, Warrenton, Virginia, in 1963 (141). The authors state that "while at present the compelling motivation may be savings in space and cost, microform facsimiles, together with means for their mechanised selection and retrieval, offer more than an alternate approach to "housekeeping problems". In support of this, the authors cite the minimising of the loss of rare and irreplaceable materials through deterioration (a role in which microforms are already relatively well established), and their use as a means of attaining far wider coverage of the world's documentary resources through acquisition of materials reasonably only available as microforms.

The authors see the continuing growth in the output of literature via conventional publishing processes as posing serious difficulties for libraries—simply increasing holdings is obviously impractical even for major libraries. Five alternative methods of copying with this situation are postulated:

1 The library maintains the same subject coverage but becomes more selective.

2 It restricts subject coverage and becomes more specialised.

3 Groups of libraries co-operate and inter-lend required material.

4 The library acquires some of its holdings on microform only.

5 To supplement interlending (option 3) facsimile transmission is used.

Recent trends are said to show that the first three alternatives are being actively exploited but appear to be reaching a point of diminishing returns for improving the effectiveness of library services. Alternative 5 (facsimile transmission) is still in its early trial stage, economics are difficult to estimate, and it does not offer attractive facilities in situations where it is not possible to make in advance facsimile copies of large numbers of infrequently used items (it is worth noting that facsimile transmission otherwise fits in well with alternative 4, to the extent that microforms greatly ease the technical problems of document manipulation by remote control at the user points).

Alternative 4 is said to be an emerging practice and probably will be used for expanding collections into new areas; there is also likely to be a growing tendency for simultaneous publication on microform. The economics of holding journals in unbound form for a limited number of years and then substituting microform holdings appear to be favourable.

In general the authors consider that for the first time microforms can be considered as alternatives to hard copy, both from the viewpoints of benefits to users and economic factors. The situation is so because microform readers are becoming increasingly acceptable, and mechanised search techniques combined with high quality image reduction techniques permit microforms to function as a new approach to information control rather than just a storage medium. The authors provide a 91 reference bibliography covering both retrieval devices and the more general aspects of library microform applications.

S. Schatz reports (330) that a microform based facsimile transmission system has been constructed and partially evaluated at Massachusetts Institute of Technology.

Proposals for packaged and desk-top libraries

The fact that microforms combine miniaturisation with low cost duplication has led to a range of activities and proposals associated with the packaged and desk-top library concepts. The terminology of this field is far from established, but for the purposes of this survey the desk-top library concept is considered to be one that exploits the "D" or duplicating proposals as set out by Heilprin (139) in that services and equipment are made available to the library users to permit the acquisition of micro-copies of relevant information in full, thus allowing the building up of an entirely personal collection of material. The services may either operate on the basis of duplicating from a master microcopy store on demand, or may be based on developments in self-service camera-processors, permitting the user to create instantly microcopies of required originals or parts of originals. Interest in the atter approach with the library field is demonstrated by development grants in the United States from the Council on Library Resources to Houston Fearless for a microfiche camera-processor and to Bell & Howell for a micro-xerographic microfiche camera (145 and 159). Widening the sphere to embrace additionally business records, the grant to Caps Equipment Ltd. of funds to develop a Kalvar camera by the British National Research and Development Corporation represents a similar approach (146).

The "packaged" library represents a new concept in information dissemination in which unabridged material selected by form or subject is systematically microcopied, arranged and supplied to users, together with an index to the collection and regular updating of the total "package".

A variety of such services is now on offer or proposed; they tend to represent an amalgam of library dissemination and publishing proper. Some, such as the Medical Research Council's project FAIR (110) and the National Reprographic Centre's proposed micro library service (111), are based on non-commercial, specialised libraries of information; another emanates from a large government department (the U.S. Patent Office (147 to 150)) as a method of publishing its own material, while a final group concerned primarily, but not exclusively, with product information (trade literature) are available from commercial publishers, notably the Thomas Micro Catalog service in the U.S.A. (151), Information Handling's "Visual Search Microfilm File" (VSMF) in the U.S.A. and Europe (152-153), the Technical Indexes Ltd. service and the Technical Information on Microfilm Ltd. (TIM) service (154) both in the United Kingdom. A final category of packaged library is represented in the U.S.A. by the activities of the Educational Resources Information Center (ERIC), in which educational research material collected at eighteen specialist clearinghouses is disseminated on microfiches.

Microform systems to meet the duplicating library concept are based on "on demand" production of a single microform to meet a user's request. Low capacity microforms, such as microfiches or eight-up aperture cards, appear to be the most appropriate dissemination media since such systems are essentially concerned with supplying discrete units of information to meet specific users' needs.

Conversely, packaged libraries consist of collections of material issued as a package in large groups; these services therefore can effectively use high capacity media such as roll film or ultra high reduction ratio microfiche (although in certain circumstances the low capacity media remain viable).

Likewise the copyright problems are significantly different for the two categories; the situation in regard to the duplicating library concept using microforms appears to be essentially identical to that pertaining to full size copying, to the extent that each item is supplied against a specific demand, the terms of the various fair copying declarations can be adhered to and a copyright indemnity completed against each request. However, G. J. Sophar (296) reports that restraints on copying are in practice as much economic as legal; if microforms lower the cost therefore they might create greater strains in the copyright situation. The packaged library using copyrighted material clearly breaches the spirit of the existing copyright laws in that it involves the recording and duplication of copyrighted material to multiple subscribers. The major aim of the proposal NRCd packaged library service is to provide an objective basis for the assessment of the influence of these services on conventional publication as a guide for any future changes in legislation.

On the question of copyright legislation, Williams (59) makes the basic point that both authors, copyright owners and librarians essentially have a common objective in communicating information to the ultimate recipient. Present copyright legislation, essentially a product of an era when printing was the normal and accepted mode of disseminating written material, is increasingly restraining the use of more efficient communications brought about by technical developments in reprography and microform systems. At the same time copyright owners clearly retain a right to a return on the products of their work. He goes on to state that, with present data processing techniques allied to a standard system of coding documents, there should be no insurmountable difficulties in establishing a system of unrestrained duplication allied to a feedback of royalties to copyright owners. N. Goodwin (297) has proposed a system for the compulsory licensing of information copies based on the allocation of a unique 15 digit number to each item. (The British standard book number system would provide a suitable basis for such a system.)

H. J. Hilton (319) is effectively in agreement with Sophar in stating that many organisations are willing to pay compensation but cannot overcome the problems of obtaining permission—it is often impossible to locate the copyright owner or licensing restrictions forbid the granting of permission. Hilton, like Goodwin, sees the answer in an identification code system. He proposes a two-part code number; the first part of five fields he claims would identify 99% of items, the second part of seven fields provides other necessary and helpful information.

The significance of the packaged library concept on libraries is complex; in certain cases (the Medical Research Council (110) or the NRCd (111)) specialised libraries themselves will be the publishers or originators, in most cases they will be the recipients—as in the case of industrial libraries for the product information services or a potentially wide range of libraries for U.S. patents on microform. In other cases, again, the services may frequently go direct to specialised departments (in the case of the product information to design offices), and particularly with the lower priced services, go to individual users who may thus have more information readily available within the specified area than has their local library facility. The services frequently include the provision of reading equipment in the package. Another factor of importance concerning these services is that they will, assuming their success with the users, very substantially increase the number of reading devices in use. The TIM service (154) is reported to involve a firm order for 1,000 PCMI readers with an option on a further 2,500—operation on such a scale has certainly never before been experienced in the microforms field; a Rank Xerox survey (155) estimated in 1964, for example, that there were then in total only 830 readers in use in British libraries.

The overall effects on libraries are likely to be three-fold: (a) the situation in which low production quantities leading to high unit costs will disappear and prices may well drop substantially for this type of reading device favoured by these systems; (b) conversely, the pressures against using the non-favoured microforms will increase; (c) the resistance by users to microforms due to the need to visit a library will become less applicable where 'popular' microforms are involved due to the wider availability of equipment.

Desk-top libraries proposals

One of the earliest and most persistent advocates of the desk-top library concept has been the Microfiche Foundation in Holland under its director, Dr. R. L. J. Van der Wolk. In (156 and 157) the case for using microfiches is argued lucidly: " . . . Users, who are increasingly lacking the means to buy what they need (due to rising prices) are placing an ever greater burden on the libraries. As a result the material is not available on the date desired and . . . the borrower cannot keep it as long as needed for his study . . . No, the classical practice of owning a handy private collection of professional literature, and occasionally borrowing from a neighbouring scientific library . . . does not work any more . . . (and this) seriously interferes with the progress of work on hand."

Dr. Van der Wolk goes on to say: "The microfiche system now enables him to start to build up a compact collection of his own to which he can have access whenever and wherever he wishes."

The desk-top concept may, as has already been noted, operate in two ways:

1 By "on demand" recording of originals by the user.

2 By micro-duplication from a store of microcopy masters.

The first method has the advantage of full flexibility and may be a complementary facility to an otherwise wholly conventional library.

However, the use of conventional silver halide cameras entails a processing delay of at least several hours in practice, the overall cost is about 5d. per page, and the system may begin to look inefficient in cases where the same items could be seen to be going through the micro-recording operations repeatedly in answer to specific requests.

Ideally, a system of this type would:

1 Give instant microcopy without processing delays.

2 Be operable in a normal library environment and not confined to photographic areas.

3 Be simple and automatic enough to permit, where needed, self service as on modern full-size copiers.

4 Additionally, the facility to make optimum use of the microfiches by adding further information in unused frame spaces would be useful in keeping costs to a minimum and possibly more so in grouping information by subject.

Desk-top libraries—specific camera proposals

None of the conventional step-and-repeat cameras for microfiche meet any of these criteria. Two development projects have been sponsored in the United States by the Council on Library Resources, and a third sponsored by the National Research and Development Corporation is being carried out by Caps Equipment in Great Britain. Additionally, the Micrex camera prototype under development by Cameronics Ltd. also appears to be moving towards providing similar facilities, and finally the "lozenge" concept by Holtronics Ltd. might also provide the basis for a suitable design.

For the "eight-up" aperture card, fully developed camera-processor models (the Filmac 1,000 and 2,000 cameras) are already available from the 3M Company. Both of these cameras produce a fully processed aperture card within 40 seconds of the final exposure. So far as the microduplication of periodical articles are concerned, it seems reasonably likely that a majority of the material would fall within the eight page capacity of this microformat. Data on the camera is given by O. Frank (298) while R. I. Riding (299) and an anonymous author (300) describe its use in the technical library of Glaxo Ltd.

The first of the Council on Library Resources Projects in association with Bell & Howell is described by W. E. Bixby (159). It consists of a microxerographic camera-processer. A prototype of this device was on field trial at the John Crerar Library, Illinois Institute of Technology, in 1965, and was described by G. H. Wright (158). In operation a book or journal was placed face downwards on the exposure platen, the 3 x 5 inch transparency or opaque sheet to receive the micro-image was placed over the reference window, the exposure button pressed, and within 30 seconds the opaque or transparency was returned with a micro-image reduced twelve times. The opaque or fiche was then positioned for the next image. Since Bixby's paper relating to the device appeared in 1962, there would appear to be problems somewhere since the device is still not yet on the market. As described, the device appears capable of meeting all four of the systems criteria proposed above.

The second CLR project was announced in 1965 (160) and called for the development and delivery in one year by the Houston Fearless Co., of a prototype step-and-repeat camera processor to use with conventional silver halide materials. The device is described by B. J. S. Williams (71 and 59) and in product information from Houston Fearless (161). The camera again is largely automatic in operation and uses a flash exposure. After the final exposure has taken place, a "discharge" button is pressed and the microfiche conveyed through the automatic processor from which it emerges as a fully processed microfiche within one minute. A successful model of this device would satisfy all the systems requirements above except 4.

The first of the British developments—by Caps Equipment—is described in the context of a business records system by F. Hailey (146). The device in this case is a step-and-repeat camera for recording direct on to a vesicular film (commonly referred to by its proprietary name—Kalvar) in microfiche or aperture card form. Kalvar consists of an emulsion sensitive to light in the ultraviolet range coated on to a transparent carrier. Because the element of ultraviolet is low in normal ambient light, Kalvar microfiches can be handled in daylight. It is also possible within the shelf-life limits of unexposed Kalvar, and providing that the microfiche is normally kept in a special envelope designed to filter out ultraviolet, to add further images to unexposed parts of the microfiche. A successful device could meet all four of the suggested criteria, although 4 (the ability to add information to the unexposed area) would depend on the length of time involved and care in protecting the unexposed areas from incident ultraviolet light.

No hardware as yet is under development for the Holtronic lozenge system—described by B. J. S. Williams (59)—but the successful development of hardware could meet all four criteria proposed above. (The Holtronic's proposals envisage a system in which lozenges of silver halide are applied to a base film sheet immediately prior to exposure. The microfiche can then be processed conventionally. Subsequently, further lozenges can be applied, exposed and processed in unused areas. Processed images would, however, be subjected to repeated processing operations as additional images were added.)

Packaged libraries—proposals

In 1962 R. T. Jordan proposed a "complete package" college library (162). His proposal was linked with the possibilities of producing a new edition of G. B. Shaw's "A list of books for college libraries". The original edition of 1931, published by the American Library Association, listed 14,000 titles. Jordan states that the projected new edition would contain 25,000 titles, with annotations and symbolisation for degrees of essentiality. His idea was that microform copies of all publications listed in the "new Shaw" would be sold or otherwise distributed from college libraries. Jordan believes that the provision of such a service with each title instantly available at all times, fully indexed on the scale of a complete major college library but at a fraction of the cost, would have major implications. Staff time devoted to acquisitions, processing, cataloguing, circulation and reservations could be devoted instead to reference and advisory service to users; waiting for time for books out on a loan would be eliminated. "New Shaw" itself would be revised frequently and otherwise updated by monthly accumulations. This would take the place of the library catalogue in as far as the catalogue coincided with the contents of the "New Shaw". The key to this concept, Jordan considers, would be the development of a personal reader for use by students. He is open-minded on the question of whether micro-opaques or microfiches would form the basis of the service. He suggests that vending machines could dispense the microforms using a code number (possibly a Library of Congress number) for access.

On the question of copyright, Jordan suggests trial runs to test the hypothesis that widespread dissemination on microform might actually encourage additional sales of books in conventional format. He makes the point that more people than ever attend concerts since the introduction of the LP record (but neglects the consideration that they pay royalties on records purchased. In fact the analogy can also be attacked on the grounds that books and microforms are both a form of record—one is miniaturised, the other not; why except one form only from liabilities from royalties?). As a less desirable alternative he suggests the use of emulsions that would gradually fog until they were no longer usable (the effect of this proposal on user resistance created by attempts to read copy which had reached an advanced stage of fogging would need consideration. While a process of this type would be analogous to lending, it must be remembered that there is a question on whether lending should itself be liable to royalties). Jordan states that libraries should never confine themselves exclusively to the complete package and perhaps becomes excessively conservative by suggesting that libraries should not reduce their expenditure for hard bound books since this would invalidate the earlier arguments about staff released for more creative duties. Jordan goes on to state that many organisations are moving towards his concept by their use of microforms for dissemination; he cites Bell Telephone Laboratories, Merck Sharp & Dohme Laboratories, ASTI (now the Defense Documentation Center) and the United States Air Force.

A. S. Tauber and W. C. Myers, then of the National Cash Register Company, have a broadly similar concept to that of Jordan in reviewing the potential applications of their PCMI process for producing microfiches at ultra high reductions of between 100 and 250 x (164). They refer to Heilprin's theories and suggest that, since one 3 x 5 inch PCMI microfiche can contain 8-10 average sized books, complete libraries could be built up and requestors could receive hard copy print out or duplicate microfiches and every branch library could maintain a major collection. They see copyright as the only major difficulty (the acquisition by the National Cash Register Co. of the Microcard Corporation, a major supplier of microforms to libraries, may be interpretable as a move towards implementing Tauber's concept.) The acceptance factors involved will soon be assessable as TIM Ltd. produce their product information service on PCMI microfiche (154 and 287).

A similar although far more detailed concept involving PCMI is proposed in a report from the Department of Computer Science, University of Illinois. The proposal (301) for an information resources centre envisages a range of facilities involving computer consoles, audio visual displays and an automated library. The library would be on seven inch PCMI discs, initial selection of which would be by a modified juke box selector. It is suggested that each selector unit of 5ft. x 2ft. x $1\frac{1}{2}$ft. could hold 1,600 average books and that the units could be built up on a modular basis from ten to ten thousand in number; the coverage for a typical major discipline is thought to amount to 100,000 books needing approximately 65 such units.

In the United Kingdom two subject oriented packaged library services are in the process of being established.

A. G. A. Pickford (110) describes the Medical Research Council's Project FAIR (an acronym for fast access information retrieval). This will involve the production of a packaged library covering bio-medical engineering to be sent out to roughly 180 subscribers. The package will consist of a microfiche library together with a co-ordinate index. Material will be extracted from books, pamphlets and periodicals. One of the specific aims is to test the practicability of setting up a desk-top packaged library for use by individuals. It was intended to create the master microfiches by stripping up from 16mm roll produced on a rotary camera (since the paper was written considerations of quality have led us to the use of a planetary camera instead). Diazo duplicates were to be used for dissemination.

At the Reprographic Technology Symposium held in London in 1967, G. H. Wright (111) outlined similar proposals to provide packaged library systems by the National Reprographic Centre for documentation. The service was to cover the microforms field and to be divided into product information and general information sections. He commented that "we should persuade those who preach micro recording to receive what they preach"!

The activities of the U.S. Patent Office in the field are described in detail by H. Mueller-Saala (150), while the service is additionally broadly outlined (147-149). The intention is to microrecord all U.S. Patents issued since 1790—a total of 3.25 million—and to publish them on "eight-up" aperture cards or, alternatively, as print outs from the microcopy master file. The selection of the "eight-up" aperture card instead of the microfiche is an interesting one; the decision was based on the fact that 75% of the patents are shorter than six pages. The wide scope for machine sorting, interpreting and similar processes tends to favour the "eight-up" aperture card in circumstances where the average number of pages per bibliographic unit is within its capacity. Complete subject groups of patents will be available on diazo duplicate aperture cards. The new service will be operational in June, 1968. The overall advantages are: (a) A faster service—demands for hard copy should be met within four hours for callers or should be in the post within 24 hours. (The cost of hard copies will be 50c each.) (b) Annual savings in operating expenses of $500,000. (c) Space savings—the present store covers 2½ acres. The system in operation makes extensive use of computer and tape control facilities to punch the duplicate aperture cards. The completed duplicate cards are sorted into subject order in a nine-stage sorting operation. The influence of American Government practice in establishing microform systems in the engineering drawing and technical reports fields has been enormous and widely copied. It was predictable, therefore, that similar systems would be adopted by the patent departments of other countries and this has largely been confirmed by H. Pfeffer (302), who reports that the Committee for International Co-operation in Information Retrieval among Examining Patent Offices (ICIREPAT) unanimously adopted the "eight-up" aperture card at a meeting in September, 1967.

The other packaged library services (Thomas Micro-Catolog (151), VSMF (152-153) and TIM (154) are additionally a new form of commercial publishing and will be reviewed in detail as such in the next chapter.

CHAPTER 5

ORIGINAL PUBLICATION ON MICROFORM

This chapter deals with the microform based publishing systems, their future significance and present trends. The term "publishing" is intended to include internal publishing—that is publishing or dissemination within an organisation or group of organisations (of which the distribution of aircraft maintenance manuals on microform is an example). Internal publishing has been included because many of the cost and equipment considerations are similar.

The chapter confines itself to original publication on microforms, that is to those publishing applications where the microform is either the only vehicle of publication or is offered more or less simultaneously with full sized copy as an optional alternative. Excluded from the chapter are the retrospective publishing systems in which microforms are used effectively as a re-issuing medium for items which originally appeared in conventional form. Retrospective publication on microforms has already been dealt with on pages 43-49. The distinction between the two modes of micro-publication reflects a difference in underlying concept, and often also in practice.

The major difference in concept lies in the fact that microforms as a method of re-issuing material are user-propagated in that the publisher of the document in its original form had no intention of, and made no allowances for, micro-publication. Microforms in this area came into use for reasons dissociated with the original publication and publisher. These reasons related to the use of microforms for re-issuing out of print or rare works, for preservation, as a low cost method of storage, or as a low cost method of copying. All of these reasons are user-generated and carried out either by the user organisations (libraries) or by commercial agencies acting on their behalf and spreading the costs between customers. Generally, any benefits derived by publishers from re-issue on microform (frequently there are none since a substantial percentage are out of copyright) are purely incidental and play no part in the original publishing decisions.

Original publishing on microform is, however, publisher propagated. It will be shown below that the publishers concerned see considerable potential benefits in the use of microforms: lower publication costs, avoidance of edition size problems, faster and lower cost distribution, the facility for packaged services, ease of updating. In short, the decision to use microforms has moved backwards along the communication link from users and their agents to the publishers and theirs. Since the function of publishers is to serve users, none of the above needs to imply that removal of the responsibility from the user to the publisher necessarily implies that no benefits accrue to the latter, but it does indicate that the decision as to whether or not to use microforms is, and will be increasingly, out of the users' hands. In future the publishers will set the pace; the fact that one system in the process of being established began life with a firm order for 1,000 readers and an option on a further 2,500 indicates that it may well quicken drastically.

There are signs, too, of differences in practice. The 35mm roll film, by far the most popular medium for retrospective publication, has so far failed to gain any significant applications as a medium for original publication. Of the two alternatives used for retrospective publishing—micro-opaques and micro-fiches—the former, after a promising start as the medium for official publishing by some government departments, has now been discarded for original publishing, while the latter, in a variety of internal and external formats, is clearly a major, if not the major, contender as the most widely used original micro-publishing medium. Some competition to the microfiche is forthcoming over a more limited range from the "eight-up" aperture card, while original publishing on roll film has become the prerogative of 16mm, and the reel of film is giving way to the cassette.

A final point of difference remains. While the survey on pages 43-49 on retrospective publishing revealed a relatively long standing, steadily expanding range of activities (which nevertheless would appear to have disappointed the projections made by Fremont Rider (63)), the survey of original publishing activities reveals one enormous non-commercial activity (the U.S. Government) underway, together with a handful of library based and commercial activities. The remainder are projected or proposed services, the ultimate progress of which can only be guessed at.

Nevertheless, in view of the diversity of effort and the status of many of the organisations taking part, it will be surprising if progress is not substantial relative to the previous level of activity.

Microforms in general a publishing medium

S. Rice, of University Microfilms Inc., in a strangely titled paper "Publishing in the Microforms" (174), makes interesting comparisons between conventional book publishing and book publishing on micro-forms. He states that in the printing industry the size of the edition is in inverse proportion to the price per copy; the larger the edition, the lower the price per copy. Consequently there is a tendency to increase edition size, but if a miscalculation is made, advertising costs will mount in an effort to move the stock; remaindering or storage of unsold copies is expensive and justifies every effort to avoid it by the sales and advertising departments. For these reasons books are normally marked up to three or four times the out of pocket editorial and printing expenses to arrive at the retail price to the consumer.

He goes on to say that the possibilities of producing books on demand forms the basis for much of the micro-publishing going on today. It does not eliminate all the risks—the micro-publisher still has to estimate the number of sales over which the cost of making the master negative should be spread, but it minimises them, storage costs become negligible, distribution costs can be kept low by advertising and selling by direct mail. In practice, prices for positive 35mm roll range from $\frac{3}{4}$c to 1c per page—this compares favourably with the average price for trade books (in 1961) of $5.24 (the average page length per book would have been an interesting additional statistic, but on the basis of the figures quoted a microfilmed book would exceed 524 pages before it reached the average price).

Microfiches as a publishing medium

An early proposal for the use of microfiches as a publishing medium was published in Mainz, Germany, in January, 1940, by Professor Ch. H. Kleukens and Dr. J. Goebel (166). The title of this little publication (now available on microfiche from Mikrocopie Verlag) "Handwriting, type, microcopy" is in itself an indication of the authors' concept of microfiches as the third stage of development in communication processes. At stage one (writing) man first acquired the ability to communicate ideas on paper; at stage two (printing) he first acquired the ability to multiply and disseminate communications in large quantities; finally, stage three (microcopying) first permitted economic short run duplication of communications. More recent developments have done nothing to invalidate the authors' original concepts. Short run duplication at low cost remains a significant attribute of microfiches, particularly given acceptance of the idea that short run duplication, "on demand" duplication, and the problems of edition size are all closely related problems. On the first point all but literary and religious classics are likely to become "short run" publications at some stage in their life when demand continues only at a trickle and the remaining stocks have been fully used. Furthermore, a high level of demand spread over a long period, or a level of demand difficult to anticipate, tend to indicate the need for "on demand" publication rather than a stock holding policy—patents are a typical example as demonstrated by H. Mueller-Saala (150). It is interesting to note the lapse in time between the Kleukens and Goebel proposal (January 1940) and its implementation on a large scale which arguably began in 1963 when the U.S. Government commenced publishing technical reports on microfiches.

Dr. L. J. Van der Wolk in (167) relates that microfiches made little progress in Germany after the 1939-1945 war, and that Dr. Goebel moved to Holland in 1948 where it became more readily accepted (as evidence of this he stated that seven of the eleven university libraries in Holland in 1959 had step-and-repeat cameras). He states that the microfiche has become a mass dissemination media following its adoption by the U.S. Government. The date of this can be allocated to October, 1963, when the first National Microfilm Association microfiche standard (168) was published.

During the congress of the National Microfilm Association in 1964, A. L. Baptie (169) of the Microcard Corporation outlined the potential of the microfiche as a publishing medium. He considered that its previously leisurely rate of development (he, in fact, traced the original proposal to a paper given in 1906 to the International Congress on Documentation by R. Goldschmidt and P. Otlet) was due to two factors (a) it was treated as a form of copying rather than publishing and dissemination; (b) it was treated as another form of book. This latter point, Baptie claimed, is . . . "almost totally wrong. The microfiche is instead a new form of publication, bearing the features of currency, flexibility, low cost, indexing ability, compactness, and many other features which the book, with all its desirable features, cannot have". Baptie's complete list of microfiche attributes is as follows:

1 Can be produced and mailed quickly and economically.
2 Total or partial information packages can be placed at the users' fingertips for quick reference.
3 Can be duplicated in the field quickly and economically as
   (a) microfiche
   (b) hard copy.
4 Master negatives can always be kept on file for the reproduction of
   (a) microfiche
   (b) hard copy on demand
   (c) offset plates.

Finally, Baptie summed up the microfiche as being "a simple, flexible microform that offers wide applications in areas not now being served by any other microform or by conventional printing".

Baptie's projection of the microfiche as being different from, and in some ways superior to, conventional publications, appears to be in the process of recognition, if not acceptance, by the conventional printers and publishers. L. C. Deighton (170), chairman of the Macmillan Company, speaking at the Printing Week Program in New York in January, 1966, warned that "there is a parallel publishing industry furnishing copy in microfilm which at the moment is confined to science and technology, but is capable of extension into other areas of knowledge". He went on to state that it is not inevitable that books and journals will continue to appear in their present packages—carefully typed manuscripts can go on to microfiches and copies made available at a negligible investment in capital equipment; any local merchant can become his own printer-publisher on this basis. He considered that it was not reasonable for the enormous output of the Federal Government to be channelled through traditional publishing procedures—this would require capacity both beyond that of the printing/publishing industry and that of the recipient special libraries. He considers additionally that such information cannot and should not appear in printed form even in journals—it must be made widely available more quickly—and projects that it is likely that many journals will begin to appear in microform only during the next decade, as does the "Journal of Wildlife Disease" at present.

Deighton goes on to say that printers and publishers cannot reasonably complain about the loss to their businesses of information that can be more suitably presented on microform, but he then qualifies his statement by bringing in wider political/economic considerations: "The full interests of public information can be served only by private commercial publications . . . managed news from the federal establishment is not merely a threat but a reality, free men cannot willingly turn over to government the management of information in any area". Deighton has been quoted at some length as an indication of the significance of microforms (specifically microfiches) as seen by a conventional publisher. It is reasonable to comment that the media selected for dissemination seem to have little bearing on whether a government monopoly of information exists; microfiches can be and are used in both the public and private sectors.

L. H. Hattery, writing in "Book Production Industry" (171) in December, 1966, poses the question of whether microfiches will compete with printed books. He considers that it is too early to predict, but he comments that a boom in microfiches is taking place, and he notes that the U.S. Office of Education publication number 1027 is priced at $6.84 per hard copy but only 27c on microfiche. He questions what is going to happen to conventional publishing when microfiches are sold at 4% of the hard copy price. On the general question of the price of microfiches, he considers that costs are likely to be higher than 9c per microfiche, unless there is a further breakthrough in technology, but below the 50c for first microfiches and 25c for additional microfiches charged by the U.S. Clearinghouse for Federal Scientific and Technical Information.

Hattery outlines a number of microfiche based publishing operations —the Godfrey Memorial Library, Thomas Micro-Catalogs, Documentation Inc., Spartan Books, The International Documentation Center, and those of the Educational Resources Information Center (ERIC).

P. Herbert, a British consultant (173), considers that the most significant attributes of microfiches are the low costs of production, collation and distribution. Nevertheless, unless quantities are large, he considers that microfiche publishing is not a "do it yourself" operation since the capital costs of equipment are high; as example he quotes prices of step-and-repeat cameras as ranging from £2,000 to £15,000 and processors £2,000, readers £60–£300. Prices charged by contractors for microfiches are not yet said to be stable, but 18s. per master negative is typical, with diazo duplicates priced at 6d.–8d. each.

A. S. Tauber (172) makes a series of points on microfiches: (a) Where they are to be used manually the format must be a size that fits the human hand. (b) The unit record (microfiche) should fit the information packages that exist (and here he cites the choice of the 60 frame format specified by the U.S. Committee on Scientific and Technical Information (64) as a case in point). (c) He predicts that, as microfiche handling devices (readers, printer, etc.) become increasingly automated, the step-and-repeat camera will gain ascendancy over stripping methods, since the latter cannot produce microfiche to a precise grid. (This latter statement is a controversial one.) (d) He believes that present microfiche technology is in its infancy and that costs will go down as volume goes up. (e) Finally, he queries the future of microfiche using ultra-high packaging densities because they are less flexible in application and are out of the mainstream of use.

Passing over the point that elsewhere in this review Tauber emerges as an enthusiastic protagonist of NCR's PCMI ultra-microfiche system, he does indeed raise a point of major topical interest in expounding on the future of ultra-microfiches systems. Until relatively recently, ultra high reduction ratio systems belonged to the large number of processes under development in research centres. 1969, however, saw the implementation of NCR's PCMI as a commercially available product information service in the United Kingdom (see the review of Technical Information on Microfilm Ltd., on page 102) and its adoption by the British Leyland Motor Corporation for the dissemination of motor parts lists commencing 1970 (313).

In the United States the U.S. Department of Health, Education and Welfare Office of Education has sponsored an investigation at the Denver Research Institute into the characteristics of ultrafiche and its application to colleges and universities (the report of the investigation was due to appear late in 1969). Encyclopaedia Britannica Inc. has announced (317) the intention of publishing in Autumn, 1970, a series of comprehensive research libraries on PCMI, while NCR themselves are to publish on PCMI a 'Library information system' series of subject collections, each consisting of 100 microfiches and 700 books of essential source documentary and reference study materials (317).

It is clear, therefore, that within the period 1970-72 reasonably substantial bodies of material will become available on ultra microfiches and that publishers, micro-publishers and librarians will need to assess the usefulness and implications of the new media with great care.

Tauber's point (c), that microfiches should fit the size of information packages, raises the question of whether the gap between the 60 frame microfiche (mainly appropriate to technical reports) and the 3,000 plus frame ultra microfiche does not leave an excessively large capacity group uncatered for in between. A. Teplitz (344) proposes to fill this gap with the 'book fiche'—a 390 frame A6 microfiche using reductions of about 50x and a format of 13 rows of 30 columns. This format, Teplitz argues, would fit admirably the page length of the average book. He suggests that book fiches could be created on a magnetic tape-to-microfilm recorder and he estimates that the cost of a 300-page document produced this way would cost $38 per duplicate fiche. The same document produced full sized via offset would cost $925 or, on COSATI fiche duplicates, $115.

Teplitz's case appears convincing as a system. The emergence of the book fiche would present the publisher with options ranging from (a) 8-up aperture cards (for patents and similar sized documents) and 60-100 frame microfiches for reports and items of intermediate length; (b) through the book fiches of 400 frames for individual books to (c) ultra fiches of 3,000 frames for large collections.

There appear to be two potential problems with the concept: firstly the findings of Hawken and the National Bureau of Standards (outlined on pages 56-59) in which it is suggested that reductions for library material should not exceed 12x. A possible answer to this would appear to be that the Hawken and NBS findings were based on: (1) conventional recording technology from (2) originals as printed. The proposals of Teplitz allied to those of S. B. Gray (315) and S. R. Ray (316)—outlined on page 59—entail re-formatting via various types of cathode ray tube device.

Secondly the question of proliferation of equipment needed to handle the various reduction ratios and the relatively greater cost of high magnification readers. On the first point it can be demonstrated that three reader types would be needed to meet the total range:

1 Readers with 20-24x magnifications for 8-up aperture cards and 60-100 frame microfiches.

2 Readers with 50x magnifications for book fiches.

3 Readers with 150x magnifications for ultra microfiches (e.g., PCMI and Microvue).

While such provision may be acceptable to a large organisation at a centralised location, it would clearly be impractical for decentralised provision on a large scale and to individual users where the need for three types of reader allied to the relatively high costs of 50x and 150x magnification units would clearly render the system completely uneconomic. A way out of this dilemma is proposed by J. Ver Hulst (345), who suggests that the high magnification devices would be confined to large libraries which additionally would possess converter-printers to convert on demand the ultra microfiches back to conventional 20x reduction microfiches. He extrapolates costs tending to justify such a system as against an all-conventional microfiche system.

The proposal is ingenious. It may be that the future will see automatic access to large stores via a system in which all information packages irrespective of length are reduced to a single microformat by means of manipulating the reduction ratio combined with output on a popular 20x microfiche format for individual use. Such a system developed successfully would have much to commend it but numerous hurdles relating to technical, economic, standardisation and copyright factors would need surmounting first.

Another proposal for a book microfiche system places the emphasis, not on the medium as does Teplitz, but on the equipment: the system is being developed by two British inventors, G. Davies and Hedda Werth. Known as the 'Microbook' system (352), it employs conventional 60 frame microfiches but on a specially developed miniature hand-held reader with a battery powered light source projecting onto a four-inch square screen. The use of such a small screen will require the reformatting of originals to produce a line length consistent with screen width at an adequate magnification. Even so, the practical problems and the acceptability of a system entailing such a small display will need careful assessment against the undoubted appeal of a truly portable (hand-held) reader.

Original publication on microform—books

Early in 1967, Gordon and Breach Science Publishers Inc., of New York, formed a new division called Micropublications International (175 and 176). All books published by Gordon and Breach are to be made available collectively on, optionally, microfiches, 16mm reels or 16mm cassettes. Additionally, selected books are available individually on microfiches (in mid-1967 seven books were included on this list). Finally, and perhaps most significantly, certain books will be made available in microfiche form several months prior to conventional publication, and it will be possible to order the complete book or specific chapters or sections only from details given in published contents lists. Xerox "Copyflo" print-outs from the microfiches will also be available. The microfiches used for this service are produced by Bell & Howell and average 75 pages on each; reading equipment will be made available on rental where required.

In January, 1967, the U.S. Food and Drug Administration announced its intention to make two of its major publications available optionally on microfiches (177). The "Drug Name Directory" was to be published on Bell & Howell produced microfiches at $25, as compared to $300 for the hard copy, and the "Sign Symptom and Disease Dictionary" was to be published at $7 as opposed to $75 for the hard copy.

The proposals of Encyclopaedia Britannica Inc., and of the National Cash Register Co., to publish libraries of material on PCMI ultra microfiches (317) are outlined on page 80 of this review.

Original publication on microform—journals

There are a range of existing and proposed programmes for the publication of journals on microforms—all involve 16mm roll (normally in cassettes) or microfiches. None have opted to use the medium on which the great bulk of re-issue publishing of journals takes place—the 35mm roll.

One of the longest-standing periodicals appearing on microform only is the journal "Wildlife Disease", the official journal of the Wildlife Disease Association. C. M. Herman and D. E. Davis gave a progress report on this project in 1964 (178). They listed the issues to be tested in the project as:

1 Is the micro-publication sufficiently cheap to be used by small specialised groups for which full scale publications of a journal would be uneconomic?

2 Will microform publication permit the publication of papers which would otherwise go unpublished or published as abridgments only?

3 Will it expedite such papers?

4 Is micro-publication acceptable to users?

5 How does it affect library acquisition and use?

The first issue was sent out in three forms: 3 x 5 inch single sided micro-opaques, double sided micro-opaques and microfiches. Five hundred and twenty recipients responded to a request to indicate the preferred medium—47% opted for the single sided micro-opaque, 39% for the double, and only 12% for microfiches. Accordingly, the 3 x 5 inch single sided micro-opaque became the standard dissemination medium. Contributions were produced on an electric typewriter and the results recorded at a reduction ratio of 1:18, giving up to 47 images per micro-opaque. Each batch sent out was accompanied by a set of full-sized abstracts. The conclusions were as follows:

(a) 5 x 3 inch single sided micro-opaques were preferred because they were the most standard; the back is available to take users' own catalogue data, or for notes. Longevity, given frequent use, is 100-200 years.

(b) Acceptance; authors were at first hesitant but subsequently became satisfied with the results. No detailed survey has been made of users, but they too appear satisfied (it had been pointed out to both that use of a micro-medium removed restrictions on the size of articles and of tabular presentations).

(c) Reading devices; the costs were considered high—readers ranged upwards in price from $120, reader printers from $300. On the basis of "Wildlife Disease", the cost of a reader would not be justified but, if more primary material appeared in the same form, the costs would be more easily justified and would, in any case, tend to come down as production volume increased.

(d) Production costs: 80% of all production costs are composition, and this holds for microform publication too. In an effort to overcome this, author composition was to be tried—authors were asked to use electric typewriters with sans-serif faces preferably, but any easily read script was considered acceptable.

(e) Editorial: the publication was intended to be quarterly, but this was found to be impractical—flexibility was needed to save production costs, hence publication was to be irregular.

(f) Illustrations: black and white reproduce excellently—originals should be "flatter" than usual since micro-opaques accentuate contrast. (Since the publication of the paper by Herman and Davis, "Wildlife Disease" appears to have changed to A6 sized microfiches using the COSATI standard 60 frame format.)

The International Microfilm Journal of Legal Medicine (179) first appeared in autumn, 1965. In this case the publishers offer the journal "principally on 4 x 6 inch microfilm cards (microfiche), but it is available also on 35mm roll film and 16mm roll film". The microfiche format exploits the 98 frame presentation (7 rows of 14 frames) permitted in the latest NMA standard (69) and also adopts the NMA option to begin pagination in the lower left corner of the microfiche instead of in the more usual position at the top left. The journal is sponsored by the Milton Halpern Library of Legal Medicine, a non-profit making organisation. The journal exploits the low publication costs of microforms in two particularly significant ways:

(a) Authors are encouraged to submit material in more than one language and both versions are published.

(b) Copyright: since one of the aims of the journal is to publish important medico-legal material which otherwise might not be published or which might not appear for a considerable time, the publishers permit authors to retain full copyright—they are therefore free to publish the material elsewhere before or after its appearance in the journal (no mention is made of what would happen if the second publisher to whom copyright was passed then objected to the material appearing in the Journal of Legal Medicine).

The journal is published quarterly at $17.50 each year irrespective of microform required. Reading devices are not provided but general advice is given on selection. The publishers have introduced two interesting new concepts in their suggestion for multi-lingual presentation and copyright retention by authors, and perhaps may therefore be forgiven for describing their venture as "unique . . . involving a completely new idea in scientific communications".

The appearance of "Chemical Abstracts" on microfilm is of major significance because this is the first truly major information source of international status to exploit microforms. "Chemical Abstracts" is published on cassette loading 16mm roll. The microfilm file commences with the first issue published in 1908 and continues through the most recently completed volume. The service can be differentiated from the wide range of services involving the re-issue of serials, usually on 35mm roll, because in this case it is intended for extremely active use (hence cassette loading) and furthermore is virtually current since it is updated every 6-8 weeks.

A number of important features of the service are outlined in the publishers' literature (180):

1 Included with the service goes the legal right to print out abstracts required and to include the results in bulletins for internal distribution; also the need to take notes is eliminated.

2 The publishers require that the subscription should be in addition to one for the printed abstracts. The reasons for this are said to be that the printed abstracts will be needed for current information since they are issued on a weekly basis, also that the printed edition is needed to have access to the issue and volume indexes. (Both of these arguments look very ingenuous; the first issue—the greatest currency of the printed service—is one that the users would be better qualified to decide upon; while the second—the printed issues are needed to have access to issue and volume indexes—simply refers to a situation in which the microform edition is published without indexes so that subscription to the printed edition remains mandatory.)

3 The indexes are not yet available on microfilm, but the feasibility of using microfilmed indexes is being investigated (one effect of the present absence of indexes on microfilm is that the two versions the consumer is required to subscribe to cannot be used effectively in different locations since only one set of indexes will be available).

4 The microfilm can be purchased only as a complete set (1907 onwards).

5 Subscriptions depend on the number of users on site but range between $1,800 – $2,500 for the first year, $1,900 – $2,500 for the second onwards.

6 Two editions are available: edition 1 is retrieval coded for use with the Kodak "Miracode" and "Image Control" systems, and edition 2 for Kodak's "Image Control" and "Kodamatic" (the fact that edition 1 is contained in 284 cassettes while 2 is in 149 cassettes gives an interesting comparison of the effect on packing density of the "Miracode" optical binary codes).

The consumer can only speculate that the possibility of the micro-edition undermining the economics ot the conventional edition must have justified the restraints listed above.

An independent analysis of the new Chemical Abstracts service in use is provided by B. H. Weil and others of the Linden Research Library (186). The Library first received Chemical Abstracts on microfilm in February, 1965. The film was supplied in Recordak cassettes, and a single Recordak "Lodestar" reader printer was installed. Users retained the option of using the microfilm system on the printed volumes. This duplication was deliberate to assist relative advantages and problems. In August, 1965, two more "Lodestars" were obtained and the bound volumes removed from further use. Retrieval was by way of the "Kodamatic" coding on the film (the cheapest of the three optional systems in terms of user equipment).

Results were as follows:

"Look up" times

Use of the bound volumes involved:

1 Removal from the shelves (and occasional re-shelving to avoid chaos).

2 Turning the pages to the required column number.

3 Scanning the abstract.

4 Making any necessary handwritten notes from it.

Use of the Microfilm involved:

1 Removing the cassette from storage.

2 Putting it in the reader printer and driving the film to the required column number.

3 Printing out the pertinent abstracts (here the authors point out that a difference may exist as compared to the printed volumes, since the users may delay real study of the abstract until reading through the print-outs back at their desks).

The total time from both during the optional period was taken with the following results:

	Bound volumes	Microfilm
Test participants	32	7
Searches	67	11
References consulted	924	464
Time required (minutes/reference)	2.02	0.92

Later an uncontrolled study took place in which users willing to do so could complete a form attached to each "Lodestar". Forms were completed by 32 users involving 160 searches and 3,085 individual references (or 56 per working day). The time per reference was 1.24 minutes—it was noticed that users seemed to gain speed with experience, and it was anticipated that the average time per reference would drop below one minute.

User reaction

Results were as follows:

Medium viewed	Very easy	Moderately easy	A little difficult	Very difficult	Number of voters
Printed volumes	17%	80%	3%	0	32
"Lodestar" reader/ printer-screen image	25%	63%	12%	0	7
"Lodestar" reader/ printer-print out	25%	75%	0	0	7

The authors deduce that no really significant difference emerges; they consider that there was less than the usual reaction to change because of the user advantages in the microfilm system. There was no adverse reaction to the use of microfilm as such, and it was reported that two bibliographies were compiled by pasting print-outs together and making a same-size Xerox copy.

Problems

Problems reported were as follows:

(a) The "Miracode" optical codes badly affected the usability of the "Kodamatic" line codes (these two retrieval codes are no longer combined in one edition).

(b) Developer solution has to be changed every 100-150 prints or only daily if more prints are made per day. New rolls of print paper have to be inserted at unpredictable times.

(c) No one table height pleased every user, and adjustable chairs or tables may be needed.

Economics

Various assumptions were made: That "Lodestar" reader-printer should be provided for every 100 abstracts looked up per day—libraries with daily use loads below 100 could use the cheaper Recordak

"Magnaprint". (In the U.K. prices in March, 1968, for these two items were: "Lodestar" model PES 1 J £1,320. "Magnaprint" £532) but the latter was found to add 12-20 seconds per search due to the manual threading system.

Taking the costs per print into account, and including an "in library" time for users costed at $15 per hour, the use of microfilm produced lower costs throughout the range of work loads 50-300 abstracts consulted per day; in short, the economics of the microfilm system were considered favourable for well used libraries already holding sets of the bound volumes, also for libraries hesitant about shelving and floor space requirements.

It is perhaps a pity that some of the statistics quoted above are based on a rather small population of participants. The question of including the "in library" time of users as a cost factor is legitimate. In public, college and university libraries the inclusion of user time costs would be debatable and controversial; instead such factors are usually written into the systems attributes as an intangible "improved service to users". (It is particularly advisable to refer to the original paper since it is not possible to summarise statistical papers without leaving out basic data.)

The price structure of American Chemical Society publications on microfilm has occasioned criticism. L. N. Starker (340) points out that the cost per page of ACS microfilm publications is about 12 times that suggested by other micro-publishers. He states that this is due apparently to the photo-copy royalty built into the leasing cost but he points out a similar royalty is not included in the price of the hard copy edition. He also criticises the lease concept and queries whether the ACS would force the return of microfilm editions from organisations terminating their subscriptions. In reply J. H. Kuney stated ingenuously that the royalty permits users to explore the potential of microforms unrestrained by the possible impact of copyright regulations (the argument would seem to apply with equal force to the hard copy edition).

An alternative explanation for the disappointing prices of some micropublications was provided by an editorial in the NRCd bulletin (341) 'No doubt a microform edition, realistically priced in relation to its low production and distribution costs, would undercut the price of the paper edition to a point where the resultant decline in the circulation of the latter would widen the gap thus transferring even further sales to the micro-edition with the demise of the paper edition the only ultimate solution . . . publishers must decide what they are selling—information or paper?"

Although no published references in the literature exist as yet, the library service of a British Government research establishment has appointed a microfilm consultant to negotiate arrangements for the simultaneous publication on microfiches of a range of serial publications. It is intended that in all cases the serials will be available to other consumers on a commercial basis. Assuming that successful negotiations with the publishers are followed by a commercially viable level of sales, for the first time a substantial number (approximately forty) of technical and scientific serials will be simultaneously available on microfiches.

In 1966 the Society of Automotive Engineers (U.S.A.) began publishing its transactions on microfiches (198). This operation is in fact closely akin to technical report publishing, since the individual technical papers which comprised the hard copy transactions are now issued on unit microfiches. In fact the number of papers presented at SAE meetings had outstripped the traditional transactions and in 1965 (volume 73) only 10% of the total were included. Under the new system the conventional volume of transactions contains, instead of selected papers, a complete set of abstracts and acts as an index to the set of unabridged papers published on microfiches. Additionally, the microfiches can be purchased individually at 40 to 50c each. The microfiches are unusual in that, while they adhere to the standard A6 60 frame format, they are issued in a half positive half negative form. The upper part of each microfiche contains the positive microtext, the lower part the same text in the negative. The reasons for this reside in the fact that most low priced reader/printers use sign reversing print-out processes, hence a negative microfiche is needed to produce a positive print-out, while a positive image is preferred for reading the screen image. While the arrangement shows a commendable determination by the publishers to meet users' needs, it certainly highlights the need for reader/printers able to produce positive print-outs irrespective of the sign of the microform.

A new publication concept was announced in 1968 by the American Society for Information Science, entitled the National Auxiliary Publications Service (NAPS). The service caters for situations in which journal editors are faced with rejecting articles because of excessive length or, alternatively, of excessive condensation to fit the available space. NAPS provides a service in which the original unabridged material is recorded in full on microfiches. The summary article in the journal refers to the availability of a full text from the NAPS service. To use the service, depositors pay a fee of $6.50 for which they receive six microfiche copies. Requestors pay $1 for microfiches or $3 per print-out of up to 60 pages. The copyright owner authorises the centre to supply copies on demand.

The concept has obvious merits; perhaps not so much in that it removes restraints on length for authors, but that it may tend to diminish the length of printed papers routinely distributed, and substitutes an 'on demand' approach tailored to individual needs.

H. Wooster (322) in the graphically titled article "Our nervous Science Publishers", takes the concept further when he suggests that the future might see many publications become 'shadow' journals supplied to depositories for on-demand dissemination.

Although not in itself a publishing operation, J. Speekenbrink (182) outlines an interesting microfiche application in association with the publishing of "Excerpta Medica". "Excerpta Medica" is a monthly abstracting journal covering 2,000 serials; 50-60 journals are received daily and are abstracted by a panel of international abstractors. Original articles are forwarded to the abstractors which means that they cannot be available to the editing staff in Amsterdam. To overcome this problem microfiche copies are made prior to despatch of the originals, and these are used for reference by the editorial staff. Access time is considered to be one tenth of that of using a conventional system; additionally there are considerable savings in space and weight.

Original publication on microform—technical reports

What is clearly the largest primary publishing activity ever undertaken on microform (and possibly on any other medium) is that of the United States Government. A large number of U.S. Government departments and agencies are involved with the Clearinghouse for Scientific and Technical Information (CFSTI), the Defense Documentation Center (DDC) the National Aeronautics and Space Administration (NASA) and the Atomic Energy Commission (AEC) probably the major originators.

Following a visit to the CFSTI and the DDC in 1966, B. J. S. Williams (71) reported on their operations:

The Defense Documentation Center is slightly the larger of the two operations. DDC were responsible for the free issue of required material to government contractors; they despatched in connection with this activity 6,000 items per day. Significantly, in view of the fact that there is no pricing system to provide an incentive in favour of the cheaper medium, it was reported that 15% of requests were for microfiches rather than for hard copy (which would consist either of store copies of the original or print-out from 35mm roll or microfiches).

Recording was carried out on three Microcard and three Bell & Howell 105mm roll-fed step-and-repeat cameras. Processing took place on a roll-fed Pako "Pakoral" processor. Initial distribution microfiches were produced on a Technifax roll-to-roll diazo duplicator. Subsequently both the first generation silver halide roll and the second generation diazo roll were unitized into the familiar A6 microfiches using Kodak 12K cutters. On-demand microfiches were produced from the unitized silver halide microfiches on a Technifax fiche-to-fiche diazo duplicator.

Print-outs from 35mm roll of earlier material were produced on a Xerox "Copyflo" unit with an output increased from 20 feet to 40 feet per minute or via enlargements on to offset masters. Print-out from microfiches of later material was carried out on Microcard EL-4 automatic step-and-repeat enlarger printers; these machines use the "dry silver" process of the 3M Company.

The function of CFSTI was to publish and disseminate information from 30,000 unclassified reports received each year. The basic operations involve:

1 Analysis and indexing of incoming material.

2 Computer processing of this material for inclusion in "U.S. Government Research and Development Reports".

3 The publishing of the actual results in hard copy (generally of reduced size) and microfiches.

Largely similar equipment to that at DDC was used; camera recording rates of the two Microcard SR-1's were reported as being 3,000 pages per camera per eight days, rising to 6,000 for originals of the most convenient format. An increasing number of title slips to form the eye legible title strip on the microfiches were produced by computer print-out. CFSTI differs from DDC in duplicating the original silver halide roll on to a diazo roll and using this second generation film as a master for diazo dissemination copies, which are thus third generation as opposed to the second generation duplicates produced by DDC. Hard copies were produced from the microfiches card on Microcard EL 3 step-and-repeat enlarger printer. Unlike the EL-4 model at DDC which uses a dry silver print-out process, the EL-4 produced silver stabilised hard copy in a two stage (exposure and processing) operation; the output of the machine is 70 pages per minute, and it averaged 10,000 pages per day. The hard copy in web form was processed on a Kodak Ektolith 200 and cut into individual pages on a Kodak 12 K cutter. An official of CFSTI is reported as estimating the total annual production of microfiches by U.S. Government as about 10 million.

A. L. Baptie, of the Microcard Corporation, outlines (184) the CFSTI operation and provides a flow chart, while an an anonymous item (186) in the "Microcard Bulletin" in 1965 states that the CFSTI processes 50,000 reports each year, the average length of which is 60 pages, one third of these are unclassified reports supplied on microfiches to CFSTI by the Atomic Energy Commission and the National Aeronautics and Space Administration; the remaining 33,000 are recorded on to microfiches by CFSTI.

M. S. Day describes (183) the microform concept of the National Aeronautics and Space Administration (NASA). Notifications of all reports in the Aerospace field reaching NASA are made in the serial publication "Scientific and Technical Aerospace Reports" (STAR). All items listed in STAR are available on 5 x 8 inch microfiches—since this paper was written in 1964 NASA has adopted the Federal microfiche (COSATI) standard (64) specifying the A6 60 frame microfiche. The reasons for the use of microfiches are reported as:

1 Microfiches are cheaper than reprinting or facsimile reproduction.

2 Rapid production—the microfiches are available ahead of the information appearing in "STAR".

3 Readily adaptable for field use, need only simple equipment.

4 Compact storage and rapid retrieval.

5 Ability to print-out.

The 5 x 8 inch size was selected since it accommodated up to 84 images reduced 18 times in 6 rows of 14, and this was entirely compatible with the average document size of 70 pages. (Presumably, therefore, the subsequent requirement for NASA to adhere to the 60 frame Federal microfiche standard has proved a handicap). Dissemination copies were on diazo material because:

1 It is non sign reversing and therefore eliminates one generation. (This appears to be based on the premise that distribution copies should always be negatives).

2 It is cheaper and more scratch resistant than silver halide. Micro-opaques were rejected due to the limited range of readers and enlarger printers.

A complementary range of services to those of NASA is provided by the American Institute of Aeronautics and Astronautics (AIAAA). While NASA indexes unpublished and report documentation in STAR, the AIAAA provided, under contract to NASA and using similar techniques, a semi-monthly index—International Aerospace Abstracts (IAA)—to published, mainly periodical, literature. It was announced (185) that all non-copyright information listed in IAA would be available on microfiches (presumably, however, a major element would be subject to copyright).

There are indications that American Government practice is being adopted by other government and international organisations. R. R. Kepple (187) states that the International Atomic Energy Agency (IAEA) is producing publications on microfiches—it apparently found the microfiches supplied to it by the U.S. Atomic Energy Commission to be an efficient and economic medium. The IAEA microfiche operations embrace:

1 The purchase, where available, of back runs of periodicals on microfiches—it considers enlargements from microfiches are better quality than regular photocopy.

2 Its bi-monthly serial publication "Conference Meetings and

Training Courses in Nuclear Energy" is produced on microfiches directly from original data. The subscription is $3 per year including airmail postage, and the micro-edition reaches subscribers 6-8 weeks before the hard copy.

3 Research contract reports giving the results of research sponsored by the Agency are issued on microfiches only.

Work on the production of microfiches for the above services is done by an outside firm. The Agency is in the process of acquiring its own recording equipment, and following this intends to expand microfiche services to embrace:

(a) The publication of the bi-monthly "List of references in Nuclear Energy".

(b) Inter-library loans.

(c) Part of its collections of United Nations documents will be made available on microfiche.

Euratom in Brussels (188) intends to publish its reports on microfiches produced to the American Federal standard.

J. T. Salisbury, of the General Electric Co. (U.S.A.), reviews (204) the suitability of various microform media for the publishing of technical reports. In his foreword he states that until recently (the report is dated April 1965) engineering data and reports remained in their traditional form as full-sized printed pages but that keener competition and the sheer bulk of paper being accumulated demands a condensed form of presentation. He considers that the microfiche is such a form and that it is designed to replace and supplement the conventional hard copy. He predicts that, given time and a greater emphasis on mechanical retrieval, it will attain a position of prominence over hard copy reports. Salisbury goes on to outline the background to the development of microfiches—the problem of managing, distributing and using the enormous mass of information being generated under grants from the United States Federal Government. Salisbury then gives the attributes of four microform media for technical report distribution.

1 The roll film said to be commonly copied onto diazo because silver halide scratches easily.

2 The jacket microfiche which needs the same equipment as roll film plus equipment to cut the roll into strips and to insert them into jackets.

3 "Microfolio", a system for coating the edges of roll film with adhesive tape, then stripping the film down onto sheets of acetate in pre-determined order.

4 Unitized microfiche, involving the use of 105mm roll film and a step-and-repeat camera giving 60 images in a precise grid pattern; each roll is unitized into two hundred 105 x 148mm microfiches.

Salisbury analyses the characteristic advantages and disadvantages of the four methods and in the conclusions rejects roll film because location of specific documents is cumbersome, it is difficult to interfile data into its proper location, and there are dangers in processing such as film breakage leading to loss of individual frames. The jacket method is rejected due to non-uniformity and also due to the loss in resolution when making contact prints. The "Microfolio" system is reported to emerge as the most economical for low work volume (up to 3,000 pages per month) while the unitized microfiche method is claimed to give greater economy over 3,000 pages per month.

On the question of microfiche duplication, Salisbury prefers diazo because the overall duplication cycle is faster than silver; also diazo is dry and does not require darkroom conditions, but silver halide is preferred for storage since it is archival.

Salisbury provides a detailed breakdown of stages in the production of unitized and "Microfolio" microfiches, of equipment, prices and requirements, and of space requirements for the production equipment.

During a visit to the National Reprographic Centre for documentation, D. Mayer (197) described an internal report publication system for an international adhesives company involving the use of "eight-up" aperture cards. The service was intended to supplement an internal abstracting service already in operation. Reports in the system averaged only five pages in length and this was a major factor in the choice of the multi-image aperture card. Other factors were:

(a) After the initial slave card has been punched, duplicates could be automatically punched and interpreted.

(b) Using readers with 18 x 24 inch screens, the entire multi-page report can be displayed on the screen simultaneously.

J. E. Crow (342) describes the microfiche system used for over 50,000 internal technical reports at the Du Pont company. Using a Microcard SR-1 step-and-repeat camera and a Technifax processor, it was found that the material cost of producing one master and one duplicate microfiche was $0.204 per microfiche. On a similar basis labour time was nine minutes. Crow considers that microfiches owe their increased usage more to the proliferation of technical information and the problems of storing it than to any other preference for microforms against paper.

Original publication on microform—lists, indexes, manuals

This section reviews primary microform publishing activities relating to documents other than books, serials and technical reports. It embraces indexing services, directories, maintenance and parts lists, and similar types of publication published both commercially and internally. 16mm roll in cassettes and microfiches are the two microforms being employed.

Information Dynamics Inc. announced in 1968 their plans to publish the Library of Congress Catalog on microfiches. Further details of this service appear on page 35.

A commercial indexing service

The Pandex service (189) represents an interesting amalgamation of computer processing and micro-publishing. Pandex is an indexing service which claims to cover 2,000 technical and scientific serials. It is published quarterly on A6 microfiches at $460 each year (with reductions to educational organisations). The service breaks down into separate alphabetical author and subject sequences. Each entry is extremely brief, being restricted to author, abbreviated title and "coden" (an international system for allocating a unique machine readable alphabetical code to each serial title) citation. The publishers do not explain in detail the production methods used in Pandex but the microfiches as distributed appear to consist of computer output on continuous stationery micro-recorded onto 16mm roll (or alternatively produced directly onto 16mm roll via a cathode ray tube recorder) which is then stripped vertically to make the master microfiches. The end product is a set of A6 diazo negative microfiches (later issues are positives) with nine vertical columns of film each containing three columns of entries. The title strip with an opaque blue backing shows the section of the alphabet covered and the date. Each of the 27 columns on each microfiche contains about 250 entries giving a total of over 2,000 entries per microfiche.

The Pandex service is reviewed in detail by J. Martyn (201) and P. A. Richmond (303).

Directories

W. Scheffel relates (190) briefly that the West German Federal mail department uses microfiches to disseminate internally telephone number changes. The microfiches, produced by Minox GMBH, are 238 x 180mm (7 x 9½ inches) in size. C. E. Nelson, during an unpublished talk given to the Institute of Reprographic Technology, stated that the system had speeded up the German directory enquiry service to a point where there was a tendency for subscribers to use the service without making any attempt to use the published directories provided; accordingly operators had been instructed to impose a minimum waiting time as a disincentive to such practices!

In 1967 International Business Machines Inc. (IBM) began publication (192-193) of a microfiche edition of the American "Zip" code directory (a system of digital address codes used throughout the

U.S.A.). The system, entitled "Micro-zip", reduced the 1,772 page Zip code directory to twelve 6 x 8 inch microfiches. The service is updated monthly at a monthly subscription of $30 and retrieval speed is claimed to be two to five times faster than with the conventional publication. Unfortunately, very few readers other than those sold by IBM will take the unusually large sized microfiches, and this is clearly a potential source of extra expense to the user.

Maintenance manuals and parts lists

The airlines are known to be very active in the use of 16mm cassette loading roll film and microfiches for the distribution of aircraft maintenance manuals.

Pan American Airlines (194) use 16mm roll film in 3M (Minnesota Mining and Manufacturing Co.) cassettes to distribute maintenance manuals to 170 airports where maintenance takes place. Each cassette holds 3,000 pages. Eastern Airlines, of the United States (194), use a similar system for maintenance manuals; additionally they use aperture cards for details of prescribed maintenance procedures (these are punched for retrieval and refiling). Savings of $62,000 each year are claimed to result from these services. Also in (194) a projected system for British European Airways (BEA) is described. BEA's cost estimates for a Hawker Siddeley "Trident" manual produced this way are said to be £12; the cost for each maintenace unit is projected at between £700 and £800 (the cost of a 3Ms reader/printer and cassettes). BEA are said to estimate total savings in direct materials costs at between £6,000 and £10,000 each year, and the savings in manhours are incalculable. They envisage ultimately computer print-out of the manuals direct onto microfilm.

In another article on BEA activities (195) R. Riding outlines the results of BEA's initial project into the provision of maintenance manuals on microfilm. Riding states that the initial trial will involve 19 sets for use at the London (Heathrow) Airport. It is stated that a set of maintenance and parts manuals produced conventionally costs £280 and can be worn out in three months; an equivalent micro-edition costs £12 and lasts indefinitely. The revision cycle will be monthly and will involve 2.5 million revisions each year. H. W. Owen, responsible for manuals publication at BEA, is said to be convinced of the value of 16mm roll/cassette systems.

A similar 16mm cassette system for the maintenance manuals of American Airlines is described (196).

In 1969 (313) the British Leyland Motor Corporation announced plans to distribute parts lists to agents on PCMI ultra-fiches. It is stated that the intention ultimately is to use computer output microfilm originals thus eliminating paper completely from the system.

T. G. Maynard (199) describes a system, used by the U.S. Navy, involving the use of microfilm in the issuing of parts lists. The lists are produced and updated by computers, the output of which is recorded directly onto 35mm microfilm, using a magnetic tape fed cathode ray tube recorder (the Stromberg Carlson 4020). The method is as follows: The computer delivers a magnetic tape which drives the SC 4020; the computer programme has to be modified by the addition of certain functional codes, but this is reported as costing less than $400. The SC 4020 displays one page at a time writing characters at the rate of 174,000 per second. The display on the tube is a negative and the resultant first generation microfilm a positive. The microfilm is then printed-out by offset and disseminated at a total cost of 45c per master offset negative—this compares to 56.9c per page for the previous system. Additionally, because the packing density is higher, the customer buys a smaller number of master negatives to print-out on a smaller number of pages. This application differs from those so far outlined in that the microform is simply a stage in publishing process.

G. R. Clarke describes (200) a microfilm based dissemination system for the subject files of the Arthur Andersen Company. The object of the programme is "to increase professional competence within the firm by making the body of experience in the file available to each member of the organisation". The file is micro-recorded onto 16mm and disseminated in 16mm cassettes (a total of 414) to company offices around the world.

Original publication on microform—SDI systems

C. A. Merrit describes (304, 338) a general and selective dissemination of information within the International Business Machines organisation. IBM is stated to have 50 company libraries throughout the world. A technical information retrieval centre was established and this operates a selective dissemination of information (SDI) system. All documents received, other than those with copyright or distribution problems, were recorded on microfiches. The subject interests of each user are analysed in subject profile. Profiles have been allocated to over 3,500 users, each of whom received an average notification of 3.3% of more than 10,000 documents processed annually. In turn each user requests on average 8% of the notifications or 26 documents each year. Total requests for 1968 are forecast as 83,000. A punched card sized microfiche ($3\frac{1}{4}$ x $7\frac{3}{4}$ inches) is used with a frame size of 10.0 x 12.5mm and reduction ratios of 1:24. This size, considered compatible with NMA standards, was chosen because of the wide use and availability of tabulating card files in the Corporation.

K. Mark and B. J. Funderburk (336) describe a generally similar system used by North American Rockwell but it is stated that experiments are taking place into direct notification by microfiche—in addition to the SDI notice the user would receive complete texts on microfiches.

G. H. Kiesewetter (350) describes the SDI system of General Telephone and Electrics. The service includes the use of computer-readable magnetic citation tapes obtained from outside services such as Engineering Index and Chemical Abstracts. Microfiches are used to provide the full text of material included in the service. Kiesewetter considers that the supply of citations without facilities for producing the full texts has little communications value.

In April, 1969, one of the world's biggest producers of microfiches—the U.S. Clearinghouse for Federal Scientific and Technical Information (CFSTI)—announced a microfiche based SDI service (353). Microfiches of all documents announced by CFSTI were to be obtainable on automatic distribution in several hundred categories by subject or originating agency. In the subject categories it is optional to specify either all documents (both prime and cross reference) or prime documents only. The system design ensures that customers ordering several categories will not receive multiple copies of the same document as a result. The microfiches are mailed twice per month and the cost is based on 28 cents per title instead of the 65 cents charge for microfiches supplied on demand.

Original publications on microform—product information

Microform based product information services are effectively a demonstration of the packaged library concept applied to trade literature library service. Product information services restrict themselves substantially to product data with appropriate indexes to product types and manufacturers.

With the trend towards increasing sophistication in all types of product and the resultant increase in the range and diversity of the range of components which comprise the equipment, the usefulness of organised services providing the necessary data seems well established.

Component and equipment manufacturers make their literature freely available to likely purchasers but the problem of organising the resultant deluge of information has always been a difficult one. Sometimes little or no attempt is made to organise product information received; individual users acquire their own collections of catalogues. The result in organisations of any size becomes chaotic, and components are likely to be specified on the basis of catalogues that designers happen to have in their desks. At the same time manufacturers find themselves providing multiple copies of expensive catalogues to various individuals at one address.

Many organisations attempt to overcome these problems by organising a library of product information—usually the responsibility of the company library or possibly the buying department. In a large company producing complex equipment, the adequate organising, arranging, indexing and, above all perhaps, updating, can consume a vast amount of effort.

The alternatives are the packaged systems provided by a specialist publisher. The field, at least in Great Britain, is covered by a few publishers offering organised product information in bound volumes covering specific fields such as architecture. In fields where the output is more diverse necessitating, in a hard copy service, multiple volumes based in multi-shelf units, only one publisher is active—Technical Indexes Ltd. with their Chemical and Electronic Engineering Indexes. Full-sized services of this type are expensive to provide, to house and to update. Technical Indexes Ltd. in fact restrict the services to major consumer organisations only, and updating (carried out every four weeks) is by the expensive expedient of employing a corps of service staff equipped with vans to visit subscribers.

It is this latter area in particular where microforms appear to be establishing themselves as a viable product information medium using 16mm roll in cassettes, microfiches or ultra high reduction ratio microfiches.

The total costs of the service provided may be covered in two ways: by distributing the costs in some ratio between suppliers, those organisations providing data for inclusion, and the users (shared cost systems); alternatively by putting the entire cost on the user with free entries for suppliers (user-pays-all systems). This point is of fundamental importance because ultimately the usefulness of the services is related to their comprehensiveness. If suppliers are required to pay (usually on a per page basis), the service is unlikely to be comprehensive, and suppliers may refrain completely from buying space in the service or may restrict the amount entered (a 200-page trade catalogue, for example, may be represented only by a 20-page selection). There are a variety of methods or proposals for dealing with this problem in "shared cost" systems. One publisher proposed including non-paying suppliers in a separate sequence so that searchers always examined data from the paying suppliers first and could only locate the remainder at greater inconvenience. Another publisher (Thomas Micro Catalogs, of the U.S.A.) has provided incentive schemes whereby users completing and returning cards of the product categories and companies searched were rewarded in one case by a small payment (a dime) and more recently by inclusion in a monthly raffle for a popular amateur camera. Presumably data from returned cards is used to demonstrate to non-buyers of space the error of their ways.

Users must be prepared to decide upon the value they place on comprehensive coverage; it is to be hoped that competing services will permit them to exercise options in their choice of systems.

D. Kennington and R. J. Adams (334) review microform based product information services available in Great Britain. The authors consider that the systems save considerable time and are generally welcome, but that the cost of print-out can double the subscription. The authors give brief details of three systems becoming available in the U.K. (this paper was published prior to the demise of the British VSMF service).

Specific Product Information systems

Thomas Micro Catalogs

The Thomas Micro Catalog (TM-C), with the launching date of Spring 1963, was probably the earliest microform based product information system, and it remains one of the simplest in conception and the cheapest in price to the user. It is a shared cost system. The major TM-C service consists of a file of general industrial product information on 72 frame A6 silver halide positive microfiches. The microfiche store is arranged alphabetically by name of organisation. The products of more than one organisation may appear on the same microfiche. The eye-legible title strip shows the names of organisations included on the microfiche together with the row and frame number at which the data commences. Rows are numbered 1 to 6 down each side as a guide to location. To overcome the difficulties created by alphabetisation when re-filing, the overall alphabetical sequence is reinforced by a serial number sequence, adherence to which achieves alphabetical order. The key to the collection is the full-sized Product Index. The main sequence here is an alphabetical list of products heads. The terms used are fairly broad and make extensive use of inversion to obtain a certain degree of alphabetic classification (e.g. Metals; rolled, close tolerance. Housings; custom moulded plastic. Housings; plastic material. Rings; brass, bronze, aluminium. Rings; bronze). From the overlaps noticeable in the examples quoted, it may be deduced that the list of terms is mainly based on those appearing in individual catalogues with only a limited degree of rationalisation of the final list. Additionally, an alphabetical index to vendors is included giving address but not products. The service is largely restricted to American manufacturers. It does charge advertisers and is therefore not fully comprehensive. The publishers attempt to counter this in two ways: (a) by "vendor search cards" on which the user may complete and return details of searches by product category or by organisation (b) by a "custom tailored" file offer which involves the user in paying an additional charge for the incorporation of vendor catalogues not in the basic service (i.e. if the supplier does not pay for insertion, the customer must). The TM-C basic file is fully updated annually when a completely new set of microfiches are issued; at six monthly intervals a six-monthly supplementary batch is published together with a supplementary product index. A reader can be supplied as part of the first year's subscription; the normal annual subscription is $250.

TM-C also issue complete sets of American military and allied series of specifications and also the QPL directory (a list of 2,000 products meeting Federal and military specifications).

They also issue a monthly journal to subscribers "TM-C report on microfiche". This contains regular accounts of TM-C systems in use (it is, of course, somewhat promotional in outlook) and draws attention to new vendors included; so far it has failed to mention vendors dropping out (if any).

Thomas Publishing Company,
461 Eighth Avenue,
New York, N.Y. 10001, U.S.A.

F. W. Santor (202), a user of TM-C, gives details of his experiences in using the service. According to Santora the American Perkins-Elmer Company installed a TM-C system with the following benefits: (a) their holdings of hard copy catalogues were reduced by 40% (b) the girl responsible for catalogue procurement reduced time spent on this function from one day per week to two hours per week. The TM-C system was used 5 to 10 times per day with each user averaging 10 to 15 minutes.

The Visual Search Microfilm File (VSMF) system

The VSMF is a range of product information services promoted by Information Handling Inc. (153, 203). The original services appeared in the U.S.A., and similar services are being established in Germany, France, Italy, Belgium, Scandinavia, Australia and several Middle Eastern countries. The services are all based on 16mm diazo film in optionally 3Ms or Recordak cassettes. The three basic systems offered in the U.S.A. are the Original Equipment Manufacturing (OEM) file which covers components in the electronic office and construction fields, The Defense Products File for use on defence contracts, and the Vendor Selector File, a directory which is supposed to help specifically buying departments in the selection of vendors. The retrieval system begins with a full-sized product index using general terms from which the searcher is directed to more specific indexes on the film, and finally to the products required. Location of the address on the film is either by Recordak's moving code line system ("Kodamatic") or by 3M's meterage system. The service is normally supplied with the product index, the cassette based store of product data and a 3M's or Recordak cassette loading reader/printer, all on rental terms. VSMF systems also permit the individual purchasers to add their own material (lists of company preferred components for example) for internal use.

The British VSMF system was promoted by Information Handling Ltd., a subsidiary of the International Publishing Corporation Ltd. During 1967 an extensive production facility was established at Farnham in Surrey. The service covered electro-mechanical components and was a user-pays-all service costing (inclusive of 3M reader/printer) approximately £1,000 per annum. The first files went out during 1968 but in autumn 1969 it was announced that Information Handling Ltd. was to cease trading.

Information Handling Services Inc.,
Denver Technological Center,
Englewood,
Colorado 80110, U.S.A.

The Technical Information on Microfilm (TIM) system

The TIM system (154) was first announced in the "Financial Times" on 27th February, 1968. This system, which became available in mid-1969, represents a radical departure from any previous system in its use of the ultra-high reduction ratio PCMI microfiche as the publication medium. The system will be based on the use of 6 x 4 PCMI microfiches, each containing 3,000 images produced by the National Cash Register Company at a unit to be established in Scotland. It is understood that this application of the PCMI microfiche is post-dated only by an internal system to be used by the Ford Motor Company in the U.S.A. The system will cover electro-mechanical components and materials and the publishers have announced that, in addition to product information, the service will include patents, standards, references to the literature and complete reprints of major articles (presumably by arrangement with copyright owners). It is anticipated that the first issue will contain 100,000 pages (presumably occupying therefore about 35 PCMI microfiches). It is to be updated every 6 months. The store will be indexed by a full-sized keyword index referring to the location, more specific location tables, company addresses and other relevant information. The final address will be in terms of the grid co-ordinates to be set up on the frame locator of the PCMI reader. The subscription will be 50/– per week including the rental of the PCMI reader. This is a shared cost system and suppliers pay for insertion. In view of the proposals of A. S. Tauber and W. C. Myers (164) and the University of Illinois (301) for the publishing of complete libraries on PCMI, the implementation of the first commercial publishing venture on this medium is certain to be watched with great interest from a much wider field than those concerned only with product information.

Technical Information on Microfilm Ltd.,
Wellington House, 125-130 Strand,
London W.C.2. U.K.

Technical Indexes Ltd. are promoting a series of services in the fields of electronics, engineering and eventually in chemical engineering and production engineering. The services will use 16mm roll in cassettes usable on 3M or Recordak equipment. The services are basically shared cost systems but provide higher subscription options which include additionally the products of non-advertising manufacturers and appropriate British Standards. A variety of subscription options are used with the highest subscriptions being £231 for the electronics service, £246 for the engineering service. These subscriptions exclude the rental of a reader/printer (£75) or a reader (£35). The company makes a point of providing indexes and product selector charts in conventional form in unlimited numbers, thus permitting individual users to retain their own copies. In late 1969 the company produced a general purpose reader to their own design for use with the service.

Technical Indexes Ltd.,
Index House,
Ascot,
Berkshire.

CHAPTER 6

INFORMATION RETRIEVAL

This chapter takes as a starting point Calvin Mooer's definition of the area denoted by the term "information retrieval" as related to the "searching and retrieval of information from storage according to specification by subject". On the basis of this definition it becomes possible to relate broadly the possible roles of microforms in retrieval systems and, at the same time, define the coverage of the chapter:

1 Microforms can play basically one of two roles in retrieval systems—

(a) They may act as store to which access is provided by a separate search system or device; in this case the output from the search system is in terms of an address in the microform store. The search system may be represented by a card index, some form of co-ordinate index, an index in book or microform, a computer or any other suitable method. The address in the micro-store may be in terms of a reel or cassette number and frame location in a roll film store, or, in a microfiche, aperture card or micro-opaque store, in terms of an item number, author or title. Access to the store may be by manual or by mechanised selection, or by a combination of the two. (In roll film systems, for example, the appropriate cassette is commonly selected manually, but selection of the required frame is frequently mechanised.) The complete systems of this type can generically be referred to as separate search and store systems and the microform component as an address retrieval system. It will be shown later that this is the most common role played by microforms in retrieval systems. It may be considered a relatively limited function as part of the overall retrieval system. At the same time, many of the gains in speed and efficiency from an advanced or computerised search systems are lost by slow or difficult access to the store, parts of which in conventional systems may at worst be on loan or located at a distant depository or co-operating library, or at best will entail leaving the search point to walk around shelves or files to locate the cited information. Additionally, a microform store permits instant duplication of sought items either as duplicate microform or as print-out.

(b) Alternatively, microform files may combine both the functions of mechanised search and store in one operation. This may be done on roll or flat microforms by combining the micro-image of the original document with some sort of machine readable code (usually binary codes in optical form, alternatively by means of magnetic codes descriptive of the contents. Combined search/store systems have found few applications relative to those of separate search/store systems. The reasons for this will be examined later.

A certain technical difficulty is apparent in the distinction between the two types; some microform systems incorporate—usually on the first frame of a roll film—an index to the contents of the system; thus in a literal sense the search facility (the index) and the store are combined in one vehicle. However effective the searching of the index and the location of the addresses cited, they remain separate operations. These systems, therefore, are separate search/store systems since, while they may combine the search and store facility in one vehicle, they do not do so in one operation.

Information Retrieval—theoretical factors

M. Camras (205) reviews the theoretical factors in assessing the efficiency of storage and retrieval systems. He states that artificial ways of enhancing man's ability to store information began many generations ago when useful knowledge available to man outstripped the capacity of any one individual's brain. The invention of writing was a major breakthrough because it permitted data to be stored outside the brain and referred to as required. There are three factors by which the effectiveness of systems may be evaluated: capacity, density and speed. The most compact (i.e. capacity and density) systems employ a thin layer inscribed with information (for example, printed pages or magnetic tape); to optimise compactness the thin layer may be either a long length rolled up or individual sheets stacked on top of each other (as in books). Measures of the density achieved have been expressed in terms of cycles per linear inch (as in tape recordings), in bits per square inch (in the computer and information fields), but where multiple tracks are involved, or for pictures and printed materials, the best measure is bits per square centimetre. On this basis the author examines the effectiveness of common information storage media and shows microfilm to be the most efficient with a gross information density in bits per square centimetre of 10^6. Videotape is third, achieving nearly 10^5 followed closely by snapshot pictures; book pages are third from the bottom (slightly below 10^2) above double spaced typed text and punched cards (both below 10^1).

But he goes on to propose that, since the ultimate purpose of storage is availability when needed, access speed should be rated equally to density because "a machine of a given size that works twice as fast has the same output as two machines that occupy twice the space". There are said to be two kinds of access speed; data rate—or the speed with which a block of information can be read out after it has located—

and random access rate which is the actual speed of location—this latter rate was chosen as the speed of the system. The author then lists storage systems in order of merit by density and speed (DS), i.e. bits per cubic cm x bits per second. On this basis genetic systems are shown as the most efficient at nearly 10^{20}, the human brain lies fourth at 10^{11}, microfilm pictures sixth at 10^{8}, followed by microfilm of typed pages tenth at 10^{6}, computer tapes (10^{6}), book pages (10^{4}), while punched cards (10^{2}) are three places above the lowest in order of merit, computer data register and logic (10^{02}).

Finally, since total capacity of a system is the criterion, the author suggests a rating that measures the efficiency of systems based on three factors: capacity, density and speed (CDS). This CDS rating is worked on the following formula:

$$\text{CDS rating} = \text{total bits} \times \frac{\text{bits}}{\text{cm}^3} \times \frac{\text{bits}}{\text{secs.}}$$

It is claimed that this measures the efficiency regardless of size. The most efficient on this basis is shown to be the human brain and nervous system, then genetic systems (2×10^{4} bits), microfilmed pictures (10^{4} rolls), core memory (2×10^{7} bits), microfilmed typed pages (10^{4} rolls); books occupy the 8th position in order of merit, file cabinets (40 drawers of typed pages) are second last above punched cards (stack of 7,000). The author concludes that this tallies with experience—filing cabinets are inefficient, books intermediate, and the human brain outstanding. The author draws attention to practical factors which could not be taken into account; degree of utilisation, reliability and cost and efficiency of organisation by way of programming or classification.

General reviews of microform based retrieval devices and systems

Although somewhat outdated in detail (but remaining current to a surprising extent in the range of devices reviewed), the "Survey of Information systems retrieving replica copies" by T. C. Bagg and M. E. Stevens (206), published by the National Bureau of Standards (U.S.A.) in 1961, remains a major contribution to the subject. The survey restricts itself to devices which:

1 Store a large amount of material in microform.

2 Store coded index information adjacent to or mechanically linked to the stored document image.

3 Mechanically search the store, and

4 Reproduce facsimilies of the sought items.

It sees many advantages to large files and libraries in providing copies rather than originals as output; store integrity is maintained and simultaneous access permitted. Another systems requirement is for compact storage but the use of miniaturisation restricts the facility to scan manually as a method of selection and retrieval (a statement which applies without qualification to roll film files but with less weight to unit microform files with eye legible titles). The survey provides a well detailed historical account of the development of retrieval devices and traces original proposals for optical selection systems from patents filed by Goldberg in Germany in 1927, through the construction at Massachusetts Institute of Technology during 1938-1940 of the Bush Rapid Selector, to the large number (thirty-three) of projected or working devices up to 1961. Both search/store and address type devices are included. A bibliography appears as an appendix while the main body of the survey consists of a detailed analysis of fifteen search/store devices and proposals comprising:

Roll film systems

The Rapid Selector
Fosdic 2
Filesearch
Automatic Image Retrieval system
Photo-magnetic system
Videofile
70mm selector

Chip and discrete unit systems

Micro Research system
Filmorex
Minicard
Magnavue
"Is there a doctor in the house?"

Sheet and strip film systems

Microcite
Walnut (IBM)
Documentary storage and retrieval system—Staats

Aperture card systems and address retrieval systems are reviewed briefly. The bibliography, while extensive (311 items), carries no annotations even to indicate the subject of citations such as "Photographic librarian" and "More instant literature".

C. P. Bourne (207) reviews factors affecting the use of combined search/store systems and indicates the number of instances and ways in which the equipment is being put into operation. He draws attention to the paradox that, while on the one hand the technical and commercial community are faced with an "Information crisis", on the other hand very few combined search/store systems have been installed (his paper was published in 1963). In general he considers that the reason for this is that most of the equipment does not have the cost or performance factors that satisfy present users' needs. He notes that the number of systems installed is only just a little more than the number of manufacturers (ten) that have marketed systems. Most installations were in U.S. Federal government departments; only two had been installed in commercial organisations and none at all in the 2,000 colleges, universities and specialised information centres in the U.S.A. Bourne puts forward the following reasons for this state of affairs:

1 *High capital, conversion and operating costs*

Some large manual systems would show conversion costs in excess of one million dollars; there are few systems which could demonstrate direct cost savings after incurring such an expense.

2 *Performance characteristics*

There is little feed-back from existing, installed systems (many of which are in government security classified applications) on how well they are operating and what improvements are needed. As a result designers have not always developed equipment to meet users' needs. Many users could not use the equipment even if it were given to them because, operating as a complete system, it fails to provide the required performance as to such characteristics as update cycle time, individual search response time, and daily volume of search requests. Other problems may arise with ease of error correction, access for single or multiple users, ability to handle a variety of forms of input material, the inability to incorporate a variety of classifications or indexing systems.

3 *Customer service*

Many manufacturers do not provide help in system design and conversion, personnel training or service bureau facilities. There are few arrangements to provide files of indexed microforms for use on the apparatus—this would be analogous to the computer field where users can obtain other people's programmes. (Since the paper was published 'Chemical Abstracts' have become available from the American Chemical Society, coded for retrieval on Miracode equipment, but the system is used only to locate columns and therefore does not qualify as a combined search/store system.)

In another publication (208) the same author reviews specific search/store devices in detail. The Bush Rapid Selector, Benson Lehner FLIP (Film Library Instantaneous Presentation), Eastman Kodak "Minicard", Filmorex and RCA's Video-storage are covered, as also are address location systems, Recordak Lodestar with image control (a frame counting device now in relatively wide use), Ferranti

Packard Rapid access look-up system, CRIS (Command retrieval information system), Magnavox Media, Avco Corporation's Verac 903 system and IBM's Walnut.

A. L. Baptie—a president of the National Microfilm Association (U.S.A.)—foresaw (209) that microforms would be used increasingly as a computer produced and accessed store. He considered that the search and store roles are best kept separate, and pointed out that, where microforms are used as combined search/store systems, the store becomes linked to a single search mechanism which cannot subsequently ever be changed or modified.

The paper (140) by P. Scott on the contribution of microrecording to Project Intrex at Massachusetts Institute of Technology has already been reviewed in chapter four. Much of this paper is of specific significance to retrieval systems including the list of considerations for microform systems design reproduced on pages 64-65 of this review. Some of Scott's questions also are of direct relevance to retrieval systems: What is the best manner in which computer interaction with a microfilm store can be achieved? (A reference to computer-based separate search/store systems). Which types of document benefit from systems that combine documents with descriptors in machine readable form? Should the descriptor codes be via magnetic striping or in photo-digital form? Or should microform stores be of the address type only?

The paper by S. N. Alexander and F. C. Rose (141) of the National Bureau of Standards (U.S.A.) also places emphasis on the need for research into the relative virtues to the user of address versus combined search/store microform systems. The paper also contains a tabular survey of both categories of retrieval systems that in coverage is probably the most comprehensive published. Altogether 49 systems are listed. Data is given on the name, the manufacturer, status (operational, commercial, non-commercial, development or proposal), the size (by price: small = below \$10,000; medium = \$10,000–\$200,000; large = more than \$200,000), purpose, response time (delayed or immediate), integration function (on line, off line or shunt), input size, storage media, storage coding (i.e. type: electro-optical, magnets optic, etc.), storage capacity, storage density (images per cubic foot), selection (automatic or semi-automatic), access time, output, print-out time, and finally, system flexibility—broken down into "update", "change", "add" and "purge". Of the 49 systems 10 were of developmental or proposal status only (the paper was published in 1963), 31 were combined search/store systems, 16 address systems, and of two systems (both by Jonkers Business Machines Inc.) the distinction was considered not applicable for some reason not stated. A further seven systems, of which no details were available, are listed by name only. Obvious absentees from the list (probably due to the date of the publication) is the Ampex Corporation's Videotape system, and the Houston Fearless CARD system.

Systems covered in the Alexander and Rose survey and their manufacturers are as follows:

Name	*Developer or Manufacturer*
1 Army Tactical Operations Central—ARTOC	Aeronutronics Division Ford Motor Co.
2 Automatic Image Retrieval System—AIRS	Recordak Corp.
3 Automatic Image Retriever	Houston Fearless Co.
4 Automatic Minimatrex	Jonkers Business Machines Inc.
5 Command Retrieval Information System—CRIS	Information Retrieval Corp.
6 Data Bank	Benson-Lehner Corp.
7 Dept. of Defense Damage Assessment Center—DODDAC	Thompson Ramo Wooldridge Inc.
8 Document Abstract Retrieval Equipment—DARE	Micro-Data Division Bell & Howell
9 Documentary Storage and Retrieval System	Henry Staats
10 Eccetron	Marcel Locquin
11 E-Z Sort with Aperture Insert	E-Z Sort Systems Ltd
12 Fast Codes, Coded Small Images—FACSI	FACSI Inc.
13 Film Library Instantaneous Presentation—FLIP	Benson-Lehner Corp.
14 Film Optical Scanning Device for Input to Computers—FOSDIC II	National Bureau of Standards
15 Film Optical Scanning Device for Input to Computers—FOSDIC IV	National Bureau of Standards
16 Filmorex	Jacques Samain
17 Filmsort (with EAM equipment)	Remington Rand
18 Graphic File and Retrieval System	Itek Corp.
19 Hi-Speed Color Printer	Radio Corp. of America
20 Intellofax	Central Intelligence Agency
21 Keystart with Microform Inserts	Royal-McBee Corp.
22 Lodestar with Image Control Keyboard	Recordak Corp.
23 Lodestar with Kodamatic Indexing	Recordak Corp.
24 Magnavue	Magnavox Co.

25	Media	Magnavox Co.
26	Metricard Analysis Console with Computer	Thompson Ramo Wooldridge Inc.
27	Microcard System	Microcard Corp.
28	Microcite II	National Bureau of Standards
29	Microcite II, Model 2	National Bureau of Standards
30	Microfilm Finder-Reader System	Massachusetts Institute of Technology
31	Microfilm Storage and Retrieval System	General Precision Labs. Mosler Safe Co.
32	Micro Image Locator	National Bureau of Standards
33	Microlex File	Lawyers Co-operative Publishing Co.
34	Micro Research System	Petroleum Research Corp.
35	Minicard	Eastman Kodak Co.
36	Minimatrix	Jonkers Business Machines Inc.
37	Miracode	Recordak Corp.
38	Photochromic Micro-Image System	National Cash Register Co.
39	Photo-Magnetic System	Peter James
40	Random Access Document Indexing and Retrieval—RADIR	Hallicrafters Co.
41	Rap 600	System Development Corp.
42	Rapid Access Look-up System	Ferranti-Packard Electric Ltd
43	Rapid Selector	National Bureau of Standards
44	Seventy Millimeter Selector	Photo Devices Inc.
45	Unitized Microfilm System	Xerox Corp.
46	Verac	Avco Corp.
47	Video File System	Radio Corp. of America
48	Walnut	International Business Machines Corp.

E. P. Taubes (19), of Photo Devices Inc., provides brief details of the better known search/store systems but he includes one not mentioned by other authorities—his own company's RASTAR address system.

E. Herbert, in a general paper (210) on information transfer techniques, makes the fundamental point that the economic case for mechanising retrieval systems depends on how frequently the file is searched and how much time can be afforded to use, manipulate and scan the references by which the search is co-ordinated; he states that analyses of which blocks of data are most often referred to usually reveal that only a small percentage of a file is highly active, and it may be more economical to skim off this sub-set into a smaller summary record more easily (and cheaply) manipulated. He considers the most active files to be those containing records of key facts like parts lists, bank and charge account numbers, rate tables and inventory lists. (This may well be the reason that automatic retrieval devices have tended to be used in just these situations as opposed to the overall library and information centre field. It may be that in Herbert's terms libraries and information centres of the type dealing mainly with books, reports or journal articles represent relatively inactive files not primarily concerned with key facts. F. Rider in (63) states that the more advanced the material in such a collection, the lower will be the per item use over a given period—and therefore present poor cases for this type of automation in retrieval). Herbert goes on to give an example of the economic basis for a retrieval device—if a device saves 77 minutes per day of the time of a file clerk earning $2 per hour, this justifies a $1,000 machine amortised in one year. He sees the advantages of "image analogues" (microforms) as low storage space requirements, image carriers which can be manipulated rapidly and automatically, ease of reproduction combined with file integrity, ease of reading given a good reader. The conventional book, he concludes, possesses only the last attribute.

W. A. Cole, of the Eastman Kodak Company (211), attempts to draw a distinction between data retrieval (anything processed by an electronic data processing system), information retrieval (the results of work processed by an EDP system), and document retrieval (not defined); he considers that the future of the latter two types of system lies in the use of microforms. He traces the development of roll film retrieval devices largely in relation to his own company's products. Dealing with address systems, he stated that target flash techniques justified the slogan "from file cabinet to reader in 60 seconds", while moving code line indexing, introduced by Kodak in 1957 under the trade name "Kodamatic", lowered access time to 30 seconds. The introduction shortly afterwards by Kodak of cassette loading readers lowered access time to 15 seconds. Finally (so far as address systems are concerned), the introduction of electronic frame counting devices (referred to in Kodak terminology as "image control") lowered access time to below 10 seconds on average. Finally, he notes the elimination of the "cross index" (i.e. the separate search device) by the use of systems using images recorded with optical binary codes. He points out that this permits rapid access to items recorded at random on microfilm. This is a noteworthy point; it is easy to dismiss such systems as being encumbered with inflexible search codes and this may be true where the systems are attempting to offer a general subject search facility. However, where the problem is to obtain rapid access on roll film to documents entering the system in random order by one or a limited number of simple criteria, the systems possess merit. The retrieval of invoices by invoice number in a system in which they arrive in a random order is a possible example.

While C. P. Bourne (208) pointed out that most of the existing advanced search/store systems were in the U.S. Federal Government agencies, H. E. Angel (212) states precisely what is where, and briefly what it is used for. The Navy Bureau of Ships has an FMA Filesearch system, the Office of Naval Intelligence uses a STORE system for retrieving intelligence documents (this appears to be a relatively simple address system), the Air Force is using an Eastman Kodak Minicard system (described as far too elaborate and expensive for most agencies), the Central Intelligence Agency is using an IBM Walnut system, the National Bureau of Standards has the Bush Rapid Selector and the Microcite device, two other specimens of Microcite are at the Cancer Chemotherapy Service Center of the Department of Health (one used for professional literature, the other for information on chemical compounds). Angel states that the greatest potential microform applications areas in the Federal Government are case files (given as comprising 80% of Government records) and technical reference files. General correspondence files are not a good application—they are de-centralised and only in active use for a short period. Angel provides a list of problems restraining the use of microforms in retrieval systems:

1 High conversion costs which could be alleviated by
   (a) Standardisation of document sizes, colours and filing methods.
   (b) Improved feeding mechanisms in flow cameras.
   (c) Lower camera costs.
   (d) Lower unit costs for bulk work—the unit cost of 500 micro-copies is often the same as for 10.
   (e) Less costly cassettes.

2 User acceptance—their needs and work habits should be studied more closely by designers.

3 Improvements in updating are essential to further progress.

COSATI (Committee on Scientific and Technical Information) in the United States in its report on national document handling systems (213) states that roll film is an effective record for collections to which documents are added serially rather than being merged into the whole; additionally it has capabilities for automatic mechanical indexing on individual frames. It states, however, that where individual frames are selected optically or electronically, the cost per frame goes up from a figure varying between less than 4/10 of a cent to $0.10 (the mixture of fractions and decimals is as quoted) to $0.35; against that duplicate reels in all cases can be produced for $7.50 per 30 metre (100 feet) reel.

B. J. S. Williams summarises available address retrieval systems on roll film (214-215) and reviews briefly combined search/store systems.

In (71) he examines in some detail the Filesearch, Miracode, CARD, Videotape and FOSDIC devices (the latter is a data input device for computers).

M. Taube (305) considers the major finding has been that, in both the computer and microforms fields, devices developed to meet a specific application have seldom met success in general applications. He suggests that the emphasis in future should be on free systems designed to match up to a number of different uses. On the question of combining images with retrieval codes, he sees little future in constantly dragging micro-images through the selector device.

L. G. Stine (219) discusses the question of random retrieval of micro-image cards. He defines random retrieval as "the simultaneous searching of all cards in . . . a file ending with the selection of a particular desired card". He considers that random access is superior to the alternative sequential access systems. Aperture cards, he states, have not been successful as a means of automatically retrieving microfilm records and are processed on tabulating equipment on less than 20% of installations and frequently then when the existence of the equipment is justified for other purposes. He then gives brief details with illustrations of the following proprietary random access systems: Needlesort, Zatocoding, Electrofile (Acme Visible records), CRAM (card random access memory—NCR) and Randomatic. Finally, the author suggests possible equipment configurations comprising desk and rotary console, elevator file, executive desk and an automatic memory and retrieval system.

Suggested mechanisms for retrieval devices

Apart from retrieval devices for which hardware exists, there have been various suggestions for possible mechanisms:

J. O'Connor (216) suggests "a possibly inexpensive attachment for a microfilm reader to permit synchronised co-ordinate searching". The suggestion is that texts or abstracts should be recorded on roll microfilm. A second roll with full sized text should be geared to the microfilm transport; this roll would contain a series of columns and in the columns would be symbols representing keywords. In use the film and roll combination would be set in motion, and the operator would scan the roll for major sought keyword symbol. When it appeared he would scan across the columns for the symbols of other sought terms and if these, too, were present, the image then showing on the screen would be that of an appropriate item. The author deduces mathematically that the search rate could be 14 rows per second. Code capacity could be increased by various colour series of symbols. A simple idea that might have applications in a certain segment of store capacities.

B. O'Brien and various collaborators (217) illustrate in detail possible mechanisms to feed 70 x 100mm unit records past magnetic and photographic scanning stations which channel the records into "select" or "reject" compartments as appropriate. The mechanism additionally keeps the photographic surface of the record out of sliding contact with other surfaces. In a typical installation the magnetic edge code would be used for first level selection and a photographic code for second level. The paper simply proposes a transport mechanism; there are no suggestions for recording or encoding methods.

D. Silverman (218) proposes, and appears to have patented, a system called MIRPS (multiple information retrieval by parallel selection). He begins with the premise that the ideal system combines search and storage. Then he notes that existing systems fall into two types: (a) Unitary systems characterised by long strips of tape or film on reels, the reels provide for easy handling, high speed scanning and simplicity, but the overall speed is slow because the complete strip has to be scanned on each search. (b) Divided systems are characterised by small pieces of tape or film (the usual term would therefore be unitised). They can be pre-sorted, therefore the scanner does not have to search the whole store; hence selection is generally faster, but they are mechanically complicated. Silverman's proposal for MIRPS appears to be a compromise between the two: there should be multiple reels of tape or film and multiple tape handling units, but only one scanner and one camera. The scanner searches a given tape; on finding a match a special gate is arranged so that the camera is focused on, and records, the appropriate text. While this is being recorded the scanner saves time by continuing its search on the next reel (it is not clear what is done about the possibility of further matching information being on the original reel). A bibliography of 22 references is given.

L. A. Smitzer (314) in 'The art of roll film look-up' describes in some detail methods of locating images on roll film. The images are assumed to be in numerical sequence and the methods intrinsically apply to any width or length of film, with hand driven or motorised drive, on reels or in cassettes, negative or positive images with horizontal or vertical screen motion. The systems range from those which partially aid the operator (i.e., they indicate which part of the film is being scanned without the need to stop the film) to fully automatic systems. A total of ten are described, all available or in use.

Retrieval devices in operation

1 CARD by the Houston Fearless Corporation.

CARD is an acronym for "compact automatic retrieval display". It is one of the newer systems (too recent for inclusion in both the NBS survey and Alexander and Rose's survey); production prototypes have been demonstrated in the U.S.A. and Europe, and a large order (15,000) for CARD devices has been placed by Eastern Airlines in the U.S.A. (220). It is essentially a random access address system, and its most significant feature is that its store is contained on international A6 microfiches, to each of which a binary coded metal clip is attached.

The CARD system is described in Houston Fearless manual (161) and by Williams (71). The system consists of desk top units priced at $3,000 which contain in standard form 750 A6 microfiches with up to 98 frames—as permitted in the NMA standard (69). The microfiches are contained in a rotating drum, and it is claimed that any page from a total store in excess of 70,000 pages (750 x 98) can be selected in 4 seconds. The operator "keys in" the address of the page or section required on a key set on the front of the device. It could be a one-stage operation where the operator obtains the address of the exact page required from the external index or, more likely, a two-stage operation with an external index providing the address of a more detailed index to the section or "book" required, from which on a second key set the operator can key in the address of the precise page required. It could be peripheral to a computer either on the input or the output side. In the Eastern Airlines application CARD, described by J. R. Weber (337) and in (220), units will be used by the airline's travel agents to hold information on flight schedules in lieu of conventional timetables. On being given details of a client's travel requirements, the agent keys in the address of the required flight schedules, the information appears on the reader screen and the client then selects additional parameters such as the flight, date, and class of seat required. This information is keyed into a separate computer peripheral keyboard and the booking then transmitted to a central computer.

A significant point about CARD is that it brings to microfiches the file integrity associated with roll film systems—in that the microfiches are not handled at any stage of the retrieval process. Additionally, in a standard roll film system a capacity of up to 78,000 pages would require a manual stage—that is the selection of the appropriate cassette and its insertion into the reader.

2 CRIS The Information Retrieval Corporation, U.S.A.

CRIS, an acronym for Command Retrieval Information System, is one of the newer systems. It is an address system placed by Alexander & Rose (141) in the medium ($10,000 to $200,000) price category. P. W. Larsen (221), of the Information Retrieval Corporation, describes it in detail. The basic unit is said to be a desk size console containing cassette insertion and scroll (these are pieces of diazo or Kalvar film 17ins. wide and either 200 or 400 feet long) positioning mechanism.

The scrolls are divided into columns $1\frac{3}{4}$ inches wide; a 400 foot scroll would contain 2,590 such columns, each of which is made up of 12 frames $1\frac{1}{4}$ x $1\frac{3}{4}$ inches. The bottom frame contains the address code, but each frame is divided into nine sub-frames, each of which bears a discrete address number. Each sub-frame stores two pages of data 30 times reduced. Access to any page is within 17 seconds on a 400 foot scroll, 10 seconds on a 200 foot scroll. An external index which can be continually updated is used. Items can be stored in random order. For retrieval the operator consults the index and then keys in the required address code with the previous one and then moves in the appropriate direction. The selector is an electro-optical device. A sub-frame of two or a full frame of up to 18 pages can be projected onto the screen; electrostatic print-out was described as under development in 1962. Also under development was a link with Litton Industries' Micro-pixprintipix device—this would convert the image to a video signal for transmission to remote locations. It is uncertain whether there are any operational installations of CRIS.

3 Eccetron Les Procedes Marcel Locquin, France

The Eccetron device is produced by Les Procedes Marcel Locquin, of Paris. It is described in detail in (222) and included in the Alexander & Rose survey (141). It is a combined search and store device using roll microfilm. Its most unusual attribute is that it operates without a coding system. In operation, up to nine keywords are typed onto a transparent sheet; the sheet is inserted into the electro-optical reading head, the film transport is set in motion and stops when identical terms become superimposed. The simplest version requires the listing of terms in a fixed order (a very substantial restraint), but a refined version permits random order listing. Again, the simplest version merely provides a read-out of the address of the complete item (here therefore is a device which reverses the normal modes in that it provides a microfilm search device for a non-microfilm store) but the Eccetron search unit can be on line to a companion Teleccetron unit which provides a micro-store facility. The cost per unit is given as £1,500, although whether this refers to the cost of the simplest search unit is not stated. (Alexander & Rose are similarly uninformed.) The system is in use at the Bureau de Recherches Geologique et Minieres (223) where the simple unit requiring a fixed order of search terms is used and the output is in the form of locations (addresses) of documents on the library shelves. Advantages over punched cards or magnetic tape are claimed for the installation; the contents of one hundred foot (30m) roll of film at 20:1 reduction are said to equal that of 1 ton of 80 column punched cards.

4 Filesearch, FMA Inc., U.S.A.

Filesearch is a roll based combined search and store system—probably the most widely used of the advanced systems. Details of it are given in both the NBS survey (206) and the Alexander & Rose survey (141), Williams (71) reports on it, and a good, brief account appears in (226). Details are also given in two of FMA's own publications (224-225). Williams reports that the price in the U.S.A. is $200,000 and in the U.K. would be approximately £60,000 (this was early in 1967 prior to devaluation of the pound sterling). Filesearch uses 35mm roll on 900 foot reels and a reduction ratio of 25:1. Page capacity per reel is variously described as 28,000 pages (225) and 32,000 pages (141) but in fact page capacity must depend to some extent on the ratio of text to binary code. Scan rate is 6,400 pages per minute. The complete system consists of three units: an electric typewriter/card punch, a recording unit and a retrieval unit. Items are indexed with each term "tagged" to indicate its status (i.e. author, date, subject, etc.); the data on the indexing sheet is then transferred to an eight channel edge punched card (eight channel tape could be used alternatively). The original document and its coded card or tape then go to the recording unit where the former is reduced to a micro-image on the film and the latter converted in the adjacent part of the frame to an optical binary code. The retrieval operation involves encoding the sought descriptors onto an eight channel punched card; this is inserted into the retrieval unit which compares the sought data against the indexing data on the film. The selector incorporates "AND", "OR" and "NOT" logic. Output can be in one of four modes:

1 Browse—image display on screen.

2 Retrieve—a print-out is supplied.

3 Expand—a contact print of both the document and its coding is made onto 35mm duplicate film.

4 Check—used to check the contents of a film produced by mode 3.

In the sequential search system used by Filesearch, mode 3 (expand) is the most significant since it permits a system in which the random input of information onto the number 1 negative film can be broken down into a series of number 2 positive films to create specific main file subdivisions, each of which can be built up as a separate store by a series of splicing operations. Thus, while on the one hand random order input is permitted, on the other it is only necessary to sequentially search the appropriate main file subdivision using the number 2 positive film in retrieval. Inability to do this is the Achilles heel of one of the simpler derivatives. Williams (71) reported that 24 Filesearch units were in use—two of them in Europe; applications included retrieval of financial information, intelligence work and criminal records.

FMA have published a study comparing Filesearch against computer retrieval (227). FMA's main claims relate to: (a) If a sequential search system is used on a computer, the large number of matching operations require a powerful expensive device. If on the other hand an inverted system (searching descriptors for common items) is used, single searches become uneconomic. They argue also that inclusion of abstracts is expensive in keypunching, while their exclusion requires manual retrieval from library shelves or automatic search of a microfilm store involving additional equipment similar in any case to existing Filesearch equipment.

5 Filmorex, Jacques Semain

Filmorex is one of the longer established and cheaper systems. It is covered by both NBS survey (206), Alexander & Rose (141) and Bourne (208). Alexander & Rose list it as "small" costing less than $10,000. Relative to most other combined search and store systems, except Filesearch, it has sold in relatively large numbers (Bourne lists 38 operational search/store systems, and of these 15 were Filmorex). Nevertheless, there is nothing in the literature on the performance of Filmorex in practice. Other descriptions of Filmorex are available from the company's leaflet (228) and from an article by its inventor, J. Samain (229). The system uses discrete chips measuring 60 x 35mm unitized from 35mm roll film. Each chip contains micro-text in one half optical binary code in the other. Search rate is 700 chips per minute. Some versions of Filmorex use an extremely simple method of recording the binary code on the film; code cards with a pattern of black and white stripes along one edge unique to each descriptor are shingled so that the edges only are exposed, thus producing on the negative the optical binary code.

Up to 12 descriptor cards can be used with each item and the selector can search up to four (in any order) in one pass. "Prefiling" the grouping of chips into sub-divisions was advised to decrease search time. A Filmorex unit was used in the U.K. by the Low Temperature Research Station of the Department of Scientific and Industrial Research; with the closing of this station the unit was transferred on loan to the Hatfield Polytechnic technical information and library service. Attempts were made to use it on a retrieval project but in fact it has not so far reached an operational state due to electro-mechanical problems in the selector.

6 IBM 1350 Photo Image Retrieval System

The two most significant points about the IBM 1350 equipment (230) are that: (a) It is an address system that is virtually inseparable from a computer and, in fact, is designed specifically to work with the IBM 360 computer; (b) It is intended as a retrieval system mainly for engineering drawings. It is described as a single continuous on-line system intended for use with forms of information not suited to digital conversion, such as engineering drawings, maps, diagrams and identification records. The input to the system is via a convertor which accepts aperture cards at rates of up to 575 per hour and automatically transfers the image and data to a 70 x 35mm diazo film chip coded with a magnetic stripe. The 1350 permits computer control of each image including retrieval and purging of obsolete material. Output is in the form of aperture cards, each of which is fully punched and interpreted from the data on the chips; output speeds go up to 1,000 aperture cards per hour. The store is updated by purging the old images and replacing them with new images from the latest aperture card input. The minimum configuration for a 1350 system is said to be one 1351 storage module and control, a 1355 photo-image convertor and an IBM 1816 typewriter; the cost of this (pre-devaluation of the £) was said to be about £80,000 but a full complement of 1352 modules with a storage capacity of 504,000 drawings would cost about £225,000, that is roughly 9s. per drawing plus the cost of film chips quoted as 1s. 4d. each. The equipment is considered inseparable from a computer since a file with an activity rate high enough to justify the outlay would need a computer for calculating and indexing. It is intended specifically for large users operating automated production and design schemes. So far no information concerning actual installations (if any) has been published but the equipment is relatively new and appears to have been introduced in 1967.

7 Kodamatic Indexing, Recordak division of Kodak

Recordak's Kodamatic system differs from most of the retrieval systems reviewed on a number of counts. It is in effect a simple system of location on roll film using moving code lines. It would hardly be accurate to describe it as an address system in the normal sense; it is essentially a simple aid to locating a required address on a roll of film. In essence it enables an operator driving a 16mm roll film through a reader to know where he is without actually stopping the film to check. As such it does provide a useful facility on modern high-speed readers which drive a complete 100-foot roll throughout the reader in ten seconds. W. A. Cole (211) describes Kodamatic indexing. It is necessary to use a Kodak camera equipped with a series of miniature lights which record high density stripes between each image. The most expensive Recordak rotary camera—the Reliant model 600—is equipped with a Kodamatic indexer in standard form; on the medium priced model 300 it is an optional extra costing about £40. It is also possible to modify the ubiquitous Kodak MRD planetary camera. On the processed film the stripes appear as solid dark code lines which progressively change position on the reader screen as the film is driven through the reader. The film is stopped when the scale lines reach the appropriate points. The precise encoding system depends on the users' own specific requirements (the major usage is certainly within the business records field), but recently, some ten years after the introduction of the system, it has been used on a published service—edition 2 of Chemical Abstracts on microfilm (180-181) which is also coded for electronic frame count. Effective broadening of its use in published services would depend on some standardisation of encoding practice among publishers—failure to do this would require users to affix the appropriate reference scale to the reader screen before commencing a search.

8 Media, Magnavox Co., U.S.A.

Media is an address system included in the Alexander & Rose survey (141) where it is listed in the $10,000 to $200,000 category. It is described in detail by D. D. Jenkins (231). The system is also covered by Bourne (208). At the input stage the camera operator reads the address code of the document and keys the number into the camera keyboard (the encoded number appears on a digital display as a check). The document itself is then placed on the camera baseboard. The exposure operation records both the original material (at 30:1 reduction) and the binary address code simultaneously; multiple pages from the same item can be recorded with an unchanged address code. In addition to the address code, other data (such as date) may also be encoded. After processing the film is unitized into individual chips 1¼ inches long on a device operating at 240 chips per minute. The chips are then stored in capsules, each holding 200 chips. Each numbered capsule is placed in an identically numbered "nest" forming part of a tray containing 100 such nests. The trays in turn go into a file cabinet holding 10 trays. It is claimed that each Media file cabinet can store 100,000 documents averaging three pages each—said to be equivalent to 50 four-drawer conventional filing cabinets.

In retrieval the file clerk, having traced the address, simply selects the appropriate numbered capsule, places it in the selector and keys in the remainder of the address code. Each chip then passes through the selector until the appropriate code is matched, the image is then generally printed out; the search then continues till all 200 chips have passed through the selector. The empty capsule is then manually transferred to the stacking station where the chips originally removed are re-inserted and the full capsule is then returned to its "nest". The manufacturers claim file integrity (no removals, no handling of individual chips), ease of updating, purging by, for example, date selection, a print-out of any page from 30 million available within one minute; they also claim the equipment to be of low cost. Alexander & Rose list Media as "operational" in status but there appears to be no information published on actual installations. Jenkins does not state the cost per print but, in what would presumably always be a highly active file, the fact that output is normally in the form of hard copy must add considerably to the operational costs of the system.

9 Minicard, Eastman Kodak, U.S.A.

In a field hardly typified by low capital costs Minicard is singled out by H. E. Angel (212) as too large and expensive for most agencies (it is used by the U.S. Air Force). It is included in the NBS (206) and Alexander & Rose (141) surveys—the latter lists it as "large", that is over $200,000 in price. A. W. Tyler, and two other authors (243) of the Eastman Kodak Company, claim that it met a large range of information system requirements. The Minicard itself is a piece of 16 x 32mm photographic film; it has a slot at one end and the cards are suspended on a "stick" inserted through the slot rather in the way a curtain is suspended from a curtain rail. It carries digital information in the form of clear or opaque dots together with a micro-image; the available area of the card for these purposes may be in any desired proportion up to a maximum of twelve image areas (each containing a micro-image of a page of up to $8\frac{1}{2}$ x 14 inches). If the combined image/code areas exceed that of one card, additional cards can be used. The maximum code area allows 72 columns with 42 bits per column (a total of 2,940 bits)—but this would leave no space at all for micro-images. The first two columns of code are in the sorting field, which is normally left uncoded at the recording stage; then come several columns in the control field (designating file number and number of cards for example). After the control field columns come the open field columns used for subject search data—there are no limitations on order or quantity of data for this field. In the system being described six bits are needed for one alpha-numeric character—thus seven such characters may be designated per column. The Minicards are stored on sticks each holding 2,000 cards—all handling is done on these sticks; search speed is 1,800 cards per minute.

Minicards are recorded on the roll, encoding is normally from a punched tape but can be direct via a keyboard. After processing, the film is unitized into Minicards. Various sorters are available for sorting the Minicards into blocks or groups; the "block" sorter can file the cards direct on to the sticks and thus into the system. The cards may be duplicated up to, it is claimed, as many as six generations from the master file. (But this pre-supposes presumably a very high degree of resolution and legibility and the first generation card.) As the cards are duplicated the appropriate coding can be inserted into the sorting field of the duplicates, thus enabling different varieties of sorting to be applied to the various duplicate sets. This facility, together with the duplicating facility, permits the master file to be broken into appropriate subjects or other subjects by:

1 Selecting from the master file on the basis of a required subset.

2 Duplicating the selected cards together with a sorting code relevant to the particular subset.

Thus, on a given search, it is necessary to search only the appropriate subset. The selector can be controlled by paper tape input or by a keyboard. Output can be by way of duplicate cards or by print or by display on a reader screen. Two types of reader are available: a desk model or a personal model—the latter is presumably intended for individuals who have built up their own file of duplicate Minicards.

The authors claim that the system has been "designed to handle all the requirements of information searching systems proposed thus far"—clearly an exaggerated claim if only on the basis of installations in use (additionally the system seems no better equipped to permit changes in the index terms after the encoding of a document than are the other combined search/store systems).

A report from the Xerox Corporation (244) describes the development of an electrostatic reader/printer for the Minicard system based on Xerox 914 copier components. The performance of the machine was satisfactory but it was stated that it was advisable to assign specific individuals as operators, since field experience with the 914 copier had shown that the use of only one or a few operators generally resulted in the most satisfactory machine performance.

10 Miracode, Recordak Division of Kodak

Kodak's Miracode system is almost certainly the widest used combined search/store system (no published figures are actually available on the total number of installations) and it is the only one which has been incorporated in a published microfilm service (Chemical Abstracts on Microfilm (180-181)) although paradoxically, in the service concerned, it is only used to locate information by column number and therefore is effectively used only as an address system. Miracode is also unusual in that many of its component items of equipment and materials are stock Recordak items—ordinary 16mm roll film is used in standard 30 metre (100 foot) lengths housed in standard Recordak cassettes; display or print-out takes place on stock Lodestar readers or reader/printers and recording is done on modified Recordak MRD cameras.

The system is included in the Alexander & Rose survey (141) and is described by M. J. Ruterbusch (233). The term Miracode is an acronym for "Microfilm information access retrieval code". It is designed to locate items either by an assigned number or by subject using descriptors. In search type operations each descriptor is allocated a three figure code (the top limit is therefore 1,000 descriptors). Input may take one of four forms:

1 Manual code selection and manual placement of the original document on the copy board.

2 Manual coding with automatic document feed.

3 Automatic code selection using punched cards with manual document placement.

4 Automatic code selection with automatic document feed.

The codes appear on the film as optical binary codes. Each code block consists of 14 bits—three columns of four bits, plus parity and utility bits. According to Ruterbusch's report, a typical code pattern would use two columns in a fixed field, to give a six digit report number and three columns in an open field to represent three descriptors. The system is flexible in that any number of pages may be referenced to a code block while up to five code block units may be used per document. This would allow the encoding of up to 15 descriptors—assuming that none of the coding was needed for report or other assigned numbers. One keyboard (costing £315 to £440 each) is needed per column searched. Each keyboard can be set to search in a fixed field (one specified column—usually for retrieval by report or other assigned number) or in an open field, in which case the keyboard searches all columns (the appropriate mode for descriptors). The capital cost depends on whether automatic coding or document feed is required and on the number of keyboards needed, but B. J. S. Williams (59) estimated that the minimum price of a Miracode system with three keyboards would be £11,000 (pre-devaluation).

The search time per cassette is 10 seconds. Ruterbusch (233) estimates that 330 six page items, each using four code columns, could be stored per cassette. Clearly, as the published discussion on Ruterbusch's paper reveals and as Williams (59) points out, the use of Miracode in most library situations would demand the breaking down of the store into a number of sub-sets, since the necessity to search the entire store of cassettes on each search would be time-consuming. The larger the number of such sub-sets, the shorter the search. This highlights the main area of decision for such systems. A large number of sub-sets begins to create operational problems (Ruterbusch suggests that either material should be accumulated in hard copy form per sub-set category until a sufficient quantity exists to make recording it worthwhile; alternatively recording of new material could be done daily to create a random order addendum cassette which would need to be scanned with each search on the main file). Additionally, in most subject areas the greater the number of sub-divisions the more difficult it becomes to ensure exclusiveness between them, and redundancy would need to be introduced either in the search operation (by searching all possible sub-sets) or in the storage operation (by multiple recording of material and placing it in all likely sub-sets).

Nevertheless, there are many situations with less complex search criteria where Miracode can perform usefully.

Daniel (234) relates how the system is used for information retrieval in the Tennessee Valley Authority. Input apparently consists of a wide range of material from abstracts to complete books. The author states a typical request would be: "Find a journal article having a flow sheet on nitric acid plant operation thought to have been published in one of two named journals within the last ten years". Unfortunately, he gives no information on whether the subject area was broken down into sub-sets.

R. Hayter (235) describes what is probably a more representative Miracode application: the problem was to maintain an encumbrance register in a Canadian province to guard against loan swindles and abuses by recording business transactions and the liens on real property and capital goods. This was done by recording a synopsis of each transaction under the individual's name (six digits for the surname, two sets of three digits for the first and second forenames). Each synopsis included reference to an address on a second microfilm store where the original documents of the transaction were recorded. In this way a file built up in chronological (effectively random) order could be searched for required individuals' names. K. Janda (236) describes the use of Miracode in an American university for retrieving information on the world's political parties. Two sets of codes were used: 000–999 for identifying specific parties, while 00–99 indexed substantive information about the parties (again note the relatively simple retrieval criteria). Janda considers Miracode especially useful for the way it overcomes drawbacks in computer technology:

(a) It handles large amounts of information without abstracting and endless keypunching.

(b) It allows a direct man-machine interaction with a browsing capacity impossible with a computer operating in the batch processing mode.

(c) A relatively low price ($25,000) permits its use where a computer would not be justified.

(d) It possesses the same powerful search capacity.

Janda additionally gives detailed information on coding rates, capacity and other matters relating to the practical operation of a Miracode system.

M. F. Meier (332) describes the use of Miracode at the Hoffman La Roche Company for retrieving spectra produced during the analysis of potential new drugs. The operation and use of the system are described in detail and the system is considered satisfactory.

A. W. Ploscowe (333) describes the use of Miracode on the reliability assurance programme of the Douglas Missile and Space Systems division. Whenever a failure occurs, a diagnostic report is prepared which is fed to a computer which in turn outputs punched cards keyed to specific failure symptoms. These cards, together with the textual report, provide input for the Miracode system. The system is used to retrieve information on failures exhibiting similar symptoms.

H. Mueller-Saala (237) expounds on the advantages of Miracode. An anonymous author (239) relates briefly how Miracode is used in the U.S. Defense Logistics Center to locate data on over four million parts by means of an 11 digit parts number.

R. C. Campbell (238) describes methods by which a Miracode retrieval system can be linked to Alden facsimile transmission equipment. An Alden Alpur F.A.X. scanner transfers the retrieved image on to a magnetic tape. The tape may then be used to transmit the picture over standard telephone circuits to any user having a facsimile data phone sub-set and an Alden Alpur facsimile recorder. The pictures received may be recorded on Alfax paper which can be used as a master for further duplication. Using this system, documents are received at the rate of three minutes per page. Using broadband microwave facilities for transmission instead lowers the reception rate to 30 seconds per page. The author suggests the system could be applied to computer centres; users telephone the centre and follow the normal dialling code by dialling codes for the required subjects, authors or other attributes; the computer prints out abstracts of desired material and these are transmitted to the user by way of an Alden dispatch facsimile unit. After reviewing the abstracts received, the user may obtain complete facsimile texts by dialling the Alden/Miracode retrieval transmitter.

A paper in "Data Processing" (256) proposes the use of Miracode in association with the Stromberg-Carlson range of computer output recorders.

Finally, as stated earlier, Miracode is provided for column location (i.e. as an address system only) on edition one of "Chemical Abstracts on Microfilm" (180-181); edition two uses "Kodamatic". It is interesting to note that the space occupied by Miracode's binary codes in edition one results in a total store of 284 cassettes while the identical textual material in edition two used only 149 cassettes.

11 The Rapid Selector, National Bureau of Standards, U.S.A.

The original Rapid Selector was built by Vannevar Bush in 1938, since which the device appears to have been in a state of steady if not continuous development. J. L. Pike and T. C. Bagg (240) give a brief history of its development. The Rapid Selector is covered by the Alexander & Rose survey (141) where it is listed as operational but non-commercial and of medium price ($10,000 to $200,000). A detailed analysis of it appears in the NBS survey (206). Pike and Bagg make the point that the need for mechanised retrieval is so diverse that there is a place for all levels of systems from the simple edge notched card to complex and expensive computer systems—they see the

Rapid Selector as an intermediate between these two extremes. It is described as relatively fast in searching; output goes direct to the requester; each frame has sufficient capacity to be retrieved in a variety of ways; the size of code and document fields is unlimited; the operating principles can be applied to 16, 35, 70 and 105mm roll film, but it does not allow for indexing in great depth, for collating or sorting (it is refreshing to find such a detached appraisal from authors connected with the development of the device). The current format (the paper was published in 1962) is said to consist of an image with associated code area. There were 45 code bit positions, the film forming a machine word. As many words as required can be used; each contains one "sync" or timing bit (used to differentiate between image and code areas), four code word identifying bits and 40 information bits. The camera is focused on the original at a fixed reduction, and automatically re-focused on the code raster for code recording (the raster is an assembly of individually lighted compartments which form the optical binary code). The appropriate pattern is set up by a punched card input. A later type of encoder developed by Photo Devices Inc. allows originals to be recorded at various reduction ratios without affecting the raster. The current Rapid Selector (as used at the U.S. Bureau of Ships) searches a 2,000 foot film at six feet per second. The selector is encoded by means of punched cards. When a match is obtained, a contact micro-copy is made on to a second film. A particularly ingenious feature allows this copying operation to be carried without stopping the master film; when a match is obtained, the copy film, normally stationary, is accelerated to master film speed within three milli-seconds and it continues to take a contact print until a non-matching code pattern passes through the gate; the mechanism is described in detail.

C. S. Wise and J. V. Perry (241) proposed a simple coding system based on co-ordinate indexing theory which would permit the searching of up to sixteen terms simultaneously on the Rapid Selector. It involved the use of a special mask containing a 12 x 18 grid pattern. There is no information on whether any developments based on this proposal ever took place.

12 Selectriever, The Mosler Safe Co., U.S.A.

The Mosler Selectriever (242) is a random access address device which gives automatic recovery and distribution of unitized microforms or other records. It is a relative newcomer to the field and postdates the usual surveys quoted. Storage capacity ranges from 100,000 to 1,000,000 documents; the equipment is modular in concept, and storage units, which consist of parallel honeycombed walls, can be multiplexed together to step up the storage capacity. The medium used measures $3\frac{1}{2}$ x $7\frac{3}{8}$ inches; it may be an aperture card, a microfiche of the same dimensions or, indeed, an ordinary 80 column punched card.

The "mainframe" consists of parallel honeycombed walls each holding 1,000 plastic cassettes; each cassette holds 100 of the $3\frac{1}{2}$ x $7\frac{3}{8}$ inch "documents". The total capacity of a single mainframe is 200,000 "documents". (A smaller version with only one wall holds 100,000 documents). These mainframes are the units which can be multiplexed together to increase the capacity. The average access time per "document" is claimed to be 6.5 seconds. Output mode may be:

1 "Documents" delivered to the operator.
2 Transmission via a closed circuit television link.
3 Micro-duplication.
4 Print-out.

System interrogation may be through various types of keyboard or the unit may be on line to a computer. Encoding is done by notches; each card has 35 holes in seven fields of five hole positions, and single digits are represented by two-notch combinations. In selection a four digit code is used to identify the bank and the cassette; a lightweight mechanism retrieves the required cassette and passes it to the output station. On arrival at the station a set of needles corresponding to the sought coding is inserted. The cassette then passes across an air nozzle. The sought documents are free to move upwards and are removed from the cassette by twin drive rollers. They are then conveyed to a platen where they are subjected to the selected output process. It is claimed that the system is "often used" (but no information on actual installations has been traced) in conjunction with remote television monitors, each equipped with a retrieval keyboard. In some respects the equipment seems to fill a similar role to that of the IBM 1350 photo-image retrieval equipment, although its ability to output EAM card sized microfiches in addition to aperture cards gives it a wider field of application than that of the IBM equipment.

13 Walnut, IBM, U.S.A.

The Walnut system was developed for the Central Intelligence Agency (U.S.A.). According to N. A. Vogel (245) the Walnut project was based on the following premises:

1 The merged record approach (i.e. the combining of micro-images with retrieval codes) results in a slow-response system which inflicts excessive wear on the images and involves inflexibility and inefficiency in searches.

2 Roll film formats are a fair solution for manually attended systems of low activity. They are capable of further mechanisation but the approach is fundamentally inadequate for large, active systems and should be rejected.

3 Available magnetic tape based computer based memory systems do not provide an elegant solution to a multi-million record index operating in a real-time mode.

4 A multi-million system can be seriously crippled by human errors.

From the above premises emerged the basic configuration of Walnut:

1 Two related but independent free-standing sub-systems
   (a) The indexing computer.
   (b) The image file and reproduction system.
2 Random access to
   (a) The magnetic digital memory in the index unit.
   (b) To the micro-images in the image file, thus eliminating time-consuming serial searching.
3 Modular design in both sub-systems.
4 Permanent retention of images in the image file to preserve file integrity.
5 Image storage in 200 independent removable cells, each containing 4,950 one page images (inactive blocks can be removed for storage elsewhere).
6 Physical independence of the two main (search and store) sub-systems. The advantage of this being:
   (a) It is possible to search a great amount of data without scanning or passing over extraneous information.
   (b) The index can be re-classified, purged or updated without altering the image file.
   (c) As many cross indexes as required can be established.
   (d) The index is not restricted to the image file and may refer to other holdings.
   (e) The image file can be updated and purged without regard to fixed categories and file locations.
   (f) It is possible to use either sub-system without the other.
   (g) It is possible to replace either without disruption.

In practice the retrieval operation on Walnut is as follows:

1 The user fills out a search form.
2 The search criteria are read into the registers of a processing unit which causes a search of the subject section of the computerised index.
3 Abstracts matching the criteria are printed out on response cards.
4 The user reviews the cards and selects those he wishes produced.
5 The selected cards are returned to the computer which duplicates the addresses, page counts, document numbers and requestor's number on to blank photo aperture cards.
6 The blank aperture cards are inserted into the image file.
7 The required micro-images are duplicated (usually using Kalvar) on to the inserted aperture cards.

8 The user receives the imaged aperture cards which he may view on a reader or have printed-out.

Vogel concludes that Walnut applied to a technical library would "give every user the equivalent of the personal attention of an authority in his field and of a skilled reference librarian" (even so, many new skilled reference librarians must have come into use since 1962 but there remains only one Walnut).

Walnut is covered in both the NBS survey (206) and by Alexander & Rose (141). It is in the cost category of over $200,000. Parts of it are said to derive from the earlier IBM RAMAC (random access methods of accounting and control) computer.

14 TMCL, U.S.A.

TMCL (the target map co-ordinate locator) is a separated search store device for the retrieval of microrecorded maps. It is described by W. H. Carr (246) and by J. P. Ryder and J. P. Goodwald (247). It consists of a single self-contained unit for storing, selecting, displaying and printing out of maps, charts and other information stored on 70mm slides. The 70mm slides are steel framed and stored within two drums, each containing up to 1,000 slides within TMCL. Other pre-loaded drums can be stored separately if required. To retrieve the required map, the operator keys in the desired slide number on a 30 button keyboard, a high-speed motor brings the drum to the required position, the appropriate slide is then transferred into the optical system and the map is projected on to a 32-inch square screen. Two variable position cross-wires behind the display screen become visible when the slide is being projected; the position of these can be controlled by the operator to any intersection on the screen; a six digit reader for each crosswire can be set to any required figure. As the wires are moved, the distance in metres is added or subtracted. In addition to their function for reading off grid co-ordinates therefore, the wires can be used to measure off the North-South, East-West distances between any two points. The earlier paper by Carr (1962) describes how the system is used to produce electro-static colour prints using five colour separation negatives. It mentions problems of resolution only marginally acceptable. (Nevertheless, this is the only microform based device mentioned in the literature which attempted to provide colour prints). The later paper by Ryder and Carr (1965) does not mention either resolution problems or colour print-out (an electrostatic black and white printer was said to be built-in), so it may be that the former had been overcome and the latter abandoned. The device was produced to meet American military requirements.

15 Videofile, Ampex Corporation, U.S.A.

The Videofile system of the Ampex Corporation is an address system using as its medium the two inch wide magnetic tape developed for television pictures. The system is described in two papers by R. A.

Miner (248-249), an account is given by Williams (59), and a brief account is given in (250). Images are recorded on Videotape as a series of magnetic tracks made diagonally across the tape; recording is done on a Videotape television recorder. To obtain sufficient resolution for textual matter, the number of scan lines is considerably increased over those used for general television purposes. The encoded address of the document is recorded on the top quarter inch of the tape (a strip used for the sound track in conventional television work). Miner claims the following advantages for magnetic tape:

1 Flexibility—erasures and re-recordings of selected items can be made at will.

2 Permanence—recordings made in 1948 show no deterioration (this in fact hardly rates as permanence in terms of silver halide microfilm —British Standard 1153c (118) defines the lowest permanence requirement in terms of 25 years).

Input to the Videofile is via a recording station. The operator places the document to be recorded face down on the exposure platen; code input can be in one of several modes:

1 By keying in the required code.

2 By means of machine-readable addresses pre-printed on to the document.

3 By punched cards or tape.

Input would normally be into a temporary storage (buffer) unit which in due course would transfer the accumulated input to the main store. Retrieval would be a reverse of this procedure—on receipt of a signal for documents at a prescribed address the information would be transferred from the main file to the buffer unit which would then transmit the image to the user's screen; the user, remote or otherwise, would have full control over the operations of the buffer unit, the main file meanwhile being available for other searches. Since the transfer of information from the main file to the buffer is by tape-to-tape transfer (the equivalent of micro duplicating in conventional microfilm), the information on the main file always remains complete. Ampex suggests two basic systems for Videotape:

1 Random filing in which documents (such as technical reports) are stored in a serial order.

2 Ordered filing in which the information on each subject goes to a discrete address in the main file.

Videotape is stored generally in 1,000 foot lengths; documents of approximately A4 size occupy one third of a linear inch of tape. Videotape lends itself to transmission by cable or microwave. No information is available on any operational installations of the system, although the manufacturers state that one is used by a U.S. military department. Williams states that the integrity of the address system begins to suffer after 5,000 passes, and the resolution of the image declines after about 200 readings. As in microfilm practice, however, a system of master tapes and working tapes would overcome this problem at some extra expense. The minimum cost of a Videotape installation was stated by Williams to be £100,000 (pre-devaluation).

An item in "Data Systems News" (335) announces the first commercial installation of Videofile at the Southern Pacific Railroad Company in the U.S.A. The system (total cost $750,000) is to be used for the filing and retrieval of waybills (documents describing freight shipments). The total file is said to exceed 20 million with an accretion rate of 400,000 and an enquiry rate of 100,000 per month. Facsimile print-out will be the normal output medium. The system is also described elsewhere by A. Drattell (339).

16 Fosdic, National Bureau of Standards, U.S.A.

Fosdic, an acronym for "Film optical sensing device for input to computer", has been developed through a series of four marks since 1951 by the National Bureau of Standards. Fosdic installations are operational at both the United States Census Bureau and the Weather Bureau. The development of the Fosdic devices is outlined by S. Dolleck and R. E. Mullendore (251). Fosdic 2 is described in the NBS report (206). J. L. McPherson and M. Volk, two of the people closely concerned with Fosdic, describe its operations in detail (252). All of the Fosdic models, apart from mark I, are photoelectric sensing machines designed to "read" and decode certain marks on microfilmed documents and to transcribe the data recorded onto magnetic tape for input to a computer.

Its basic operation is best described in terms of the way it was used in the 1960 United States national census. In addition to the account given by McPherson and Volk (252), an account is given by Williams in (71).

The data was recorded on the original census forms largely by filling in small answer circles with a pencil; thus, if the race of the family was Chinese, the small answer circle opposite the term Chinese had to be filled in. Date of birth, marital status and other facts were similarly recorded. The completed forms were microrecorded onto 16mm roll film using modified planetary cameras. Fosdic operates by directing a beam of light at each answer circle in turn and recording the result. It consists basically of four units:

(a) The scanning unit controls the beam horizontally and vertically, and "decides" where a mark has been made, the existence of which would be recorded as an impulse on the magnetic tape.

(b) The programme tells the scanning unit what to do, the order in which questions are to be scanned, the location of the appropriate answer circle, etc. Allowances can be made for different sizes of document and the unit is programmed by means of a plug board.

(c) The tape unit provides tape transport and records impulses on the tape.

(d) The console contains operating switches, recording dials and an oscilloscope for metering impulse strength.

The original schedules may be up to 14 x 21 inches, and each could have a theoretical capacity of 13,000 answer circles so far as the operation of Fosdic is concerned, but in practice the number is restricted by the need to fit in questions and other matters relating to the physical layout of the form. The use of Fosdic was justified by the requirement for speed and by cost savings. The success of Fosdic is indicated by the following results (quoted by McPherson and Volk): the 1950 census, using card punching for processing the data involved, 200,000 man days with a peak of 300 operators; the 1960 census, using the Fosdic/Univac computer complex covered a population 18.5% larger, yet involved only 28,000 man days with a peak of 100 camera and machine operators.

The other installation of a Fosdic device is at the Weather Bureau and is described by J. F. Bosen (253) In "National Micro News"(254) and by E. C. Palasky (255). In this case the original data is on 80 column punched cards; these are micro-recorded using an anomorphic lens which gives a reduction of 43:1 vertically and 24:1 horizontally, the rectangular shape punches in the cards being thus recorded as squares. Recording takes place on a rotary camera at 800 cards per minute, each 30 metre (100 foot) holding 12,000 punched cards. Fosdic 4 reads from the microfilm at the rate of two million bits per minute; this equals a column by column examination of 2,000 full cards per minute or up to 8,000 per minute for cards with fewer columns full. The total store of cards to be dealt with numbers 400 million.

Finally, an extremely detailed description of Fosdic 3 appears in a 47 page Bureau of the Census report (257). This document also outlines briefly the development of the Fosdic machines. Fosdic 1 was developed 1951-1954 and took original documents (not microfilm) as input; it had a fixed scanning pattern and no plugboard control. Fosdic 2 was developed for the Weather Bureau and took (as related above) microfilm of punched cards as input. Fosdic 3 was developed jointly by the National Bureau of Standards and the Bureau of the Census. No information is given on Fosdic 4, the development of which post-dates the report.

CHAPTER 7

EVALUATION OF LIBRARY MICROFORM HARDWARE

One of the restraints on library microform applications as noted in the section on failures of previous systems pages 25 - 28, has been attributed to equipment deficiencies and, in that section, the views of P. Scott (61), B. J. S. Williams and G. H. Wright (66) and W. R. Hawken (100) are seen to support this view. Some of the deficiencies arise, as has been demonstrated in this previous section, partly as a result of lack of standardisation placing heavy demands in particular on reader flexibility. There remain other considerations less directly concerned with standardisation; these are reviewed here together with measures to overcome them.

W. R. Hawken provides a list (100) of sixteen common faults found in library reading equipment (see page 27 of this review). But the fact that their origin is due in many circumstances to an interplay of technical and commercial considerations emerges from a paper by P. Scott (61) who points out that, while commercial microfilm systems began with an analysis of specific requirements followed by the development of suitable equipment, libraries were forced to adopt existing equipment and re-shape alien systems. Williams and Wright (66) considered that both conservatism among librarians and their inadequate financial resources led to low level demand and failure to produce equipment specifically for libraries.

Obviously a situation where low level demand leads to use of inadequate equipment tends to be self-perpetuating in that inadequate equipment to some extent results in a low level demand.

One potential way out of this impasse lies in the publication of objective evaluations of specific items of equipment, since these educate both the user in factors to consider when selecting equipment and the manufacturer in user requirements. Two organisations—the American Library Association Library Technology Project (latterly it seems to have changed to Library Technology Program) and in Britain the National Reprographic Centre for documentation—are now active in evaluating equipment.

The American Library Association's Library Technology Project (LTP) is supported by grants from the Council on Library Resources although it must by now obtain a considerable additional income from subscriptions. The early use of the term "project" in the title of the LTP was perhaps a little unusual in that it does in fact embrace a whole range of separate activities which are established on a continuing basis; subsequently it appears to substitute Program for Project in its title. Evaluation reports on a wide range of hardware and furniture of significance to libraries; carpets, furniture and typewriters, for example, are covered. The microform equipment evaluations published have, since the inception of the LTP, been carried out on its behalf by a consultancy organisation, William R. Hawken Associates, of Berkeley, California. (Numerous references have already been made in this review to contributions by William Hawken). The LTP evaluations in the microforms field have so far been confined to readers and reader/printers. The first evaluation reports were published as a compendium entitled "Enlarged prints from library microforms" in 1961 (133). In this publication the reports on specific reader/printers and readers, from which it was possible to make prints, were prefixed by an explanation of the fundamentals of print-out systems and the processes available. The evaluations covered eight proprietary models (two of which at least—the Filmac 100 and the Microcard copier type 1—are not now in production). The final chapter consisted of a summary of findings.

Broadly, Hawken concluded that the internal (or back) projector reader/printers offered a relatively high level of automation (once the image had been located, focused and the exposure set it was only necessary to press a button to obtain a print); the external (or front) projector involved a considerable number of manual stages involving the handling of sensitized paper which in itself poses difficult problems. (Since then front projector printers with automatic operation have been produced by Mullens, in Holland—the Dagmar Twin Combi, and Caps Equipment, in England). Against this, the internal projectors were designed for the business records field and suffered from substantial shortcomings when handling the wide variety of microforms encountered in library systems.

He found the two devices capable of printing-out from micro-opaques. The British Ross reader and the Microcard copier type 1, were not satisfactory and, in a general review of the problems inherent in printing-out from micro-opaques, he concluded that a device of the highest optical quality would nevertheless be unlikely to reproduce fine detail.

Since the publication of "Enlarged prints from library microforms" in 1961, LTP evaluation activities have been concentrated on the publication mainly of reports or specific items of equipment as part of the overall LTP service. The publication of specific reports began in September 1965, and by March 1968, 20 evaluation reports on microforms equipment had been issued. Ten of these were reports on microfiche readers (or readers primarily intended for microfiches), two were on pocket viewers, three on reader/printers, two on 35mm roll film readers, while three reports gave advice on points to consider when selecting respectively 35mm roll film readers, microfiche readers and micro-opaque readers. The reports all evaluate the equipment from a library point of view, but it is reported (71) that the existence of the reports within the LTP service has attracted subscriptions from industrial and commercial microforms users. Subscription to the LTP service (which has to be subscribed to as a complete service) is $100. But individual reports are purchasable at 25% of the total annual rate to the service. The reports concentrate on equipment on the American market but the international nature of the market is reflected in the fact that 11 of the 17 specific items evaluated are sold within the British market with necessary modifications to meet British voltage requirements. LTP have also produced a number of useful equipment surveys, one of which (320) lists manufacturers and marketers of readers and reader/printers in the U.S.A. and gives essential information about each model. In November 1968 a more comprehensive survey (348) of readers on the American market was produced. In addition to giving data on some 60 models, criteria for selecting readers were also listed. LTP activities in general are described in two articles by G. T. Piez (137-138) and in annual reports (134). A brief biography of W. R. Hawken and a bibliography of his works has appeared in the Microfiche Foundation Newsletter (324).

The National Reprographic Centre for documentation* was established at Hatfield College of Technology in 1967 under a grant from the Office for Scientific and Technical Information of the British Department of Education and Science under the direction of G. H. Wright. Evaluation of microforms equipment is, in the case of NRCd, allied to responsibilities for acting as a clearinghouse for information in micrographics, for providing advisory and consultative services and for pursuing an educational programme in both micrographics and reprographics. By July 1968 the Centre had issued four evaluation reports covering two general purpose readers and two microfiche readers. Additionally, a shorter evaluation on a step-and-repeat microfiche camera had been published in the November issue of the NRCd bulletin. The Centre makes its reports series available on a subscription basis of £28 per year. Unlike the LTP, individual reports are not purchasable separately. Summaries of the findings of NRCd reports appear in the Centre's quarterly bulletin available on a lower subscription rate of £8. The summaries contain the full specification of the equipment and give the main findings of the full report. The data on which the findings are based is excluded.

* *In reviewing the activities of the NRCd the author must remind readers that he is employed by the Centre.*

The Centre does not in principle confine its evaluations to reader equipment but, clearly, in view of the length of time the preparation of each report involves (an output on average similar to that of the LTP's six to eight per year is envisaged on the present level of effort available), some concentration of effort on the most widely used type of user equipment becomes a priority.

It is doubtful, in view of the expansion in microforms use, whether the combined rate of evaluation of the LTP and the NRCd keeps up with the introduction of new reading equipment. It is useful, therefore, that in 1968 an agreement between the two organisations was concluded to co-ordinate evaluation activities on microforms equipment and to publish each other's reports selectively. Meanwhile, it is a reasonable premise that the availability of evaluative publications revealing the shortcomings of specific equipment should influence the design of new equipment in the right direction. Additionally, the reports themselves and the associated information and educational activities should promote a wider knowledge of the factors involved in equipment selection.

CHAPTER 8

STANDARDISATION – STANDARDS ORGANISATIONS

Close acquaintance with standards activities in the microforms field almost inevitably leads to the consideration of whether the process of standardisation should not itself be subject to standardisation; until recently the field of microforms standardisation was not notable for its level of activity but there is now a surge of international activity and inevitably some examples of lack of co-ordination and liaison between the various national standards organisations.

In 1967 four new British microform standards were published, a figure easily exceeding in one year the total produced in all the years prior to 1967. Fortunately, while some confusion in an area characterised by such a high rate of activity is inevitable, the key organisations are developing effective informal international links which are proving far more useful than the ponderous formal alternative provided by the International Organisation for Standardisation (ISO).

The following is a review of some major national standards. It is not a comprehensive review of world-wide activities. Indeed, the effectiveness of international standardisation should preclude major differences between national standards. It is restricted therefore to British Standards and to significant overseas standards.

The United Kingdom

The British Standards Institution

BSI activities in the microforms field are now almost exclusively the preserve of the large BS PHC 16 committee under the chairmanship of Mr. T. N. J. Archard. The committee operates through three sub-committees: PHC 16/1 on engineering drawings, PHC 16/2 with the somewhat negative title of "Documents other than engineering drawings", and PHC 16/3 entitled the "programming" subcommittee, since it was originally created to propose the future programme of British microform standards. All three committees do their detailed work by means of small informal working parties of specialists.

British microform standards in the past have tended to owe their origin to the International Organisation for Standardisation—the formal link between national standards organisations. The theory underlying ISO is that member national standards organisations will put forward their original work for consideration as an international standard by ISO. On acceptance by ISO, a definitive ISO standard is published upon which other member countries are recommended to base their own national standards. British standard 4189: 1967 (258) based on ISO/R 435 (259) is a recent example of this process. In practice this form of operation is proving far too slow for present day requirements—work on the likely ISO successor to the obsolescent BS 1371 (125) has been going on for 13 years, yet in October 1969 a definitive ISO standard is still awaited—and BSI have increasingly tended to produce standards based on work which has not achieved the ISO accolade. Indeed, two of the most important recent British standards, BS 4187: 1967 on microfiches (5) and BS 4210: Part 1 1967 (260) on engineering drawing systems, were based on work in the U.S.A. that strictly has not yet achieved national standards status even in its country of origin—BS 4187 is based on the U.S. Federal Government standard—usually referred to as the "COSATI" standard (64) which in turn owes its origin to the National Microfilm Association (U.S.A.) standard M-1-1963 (168), while BS 4210: Part 1 is based on U.S. Department of Defense military standards (261). This readiness to adopt useful standards irrespective of their source by the BSI PHC 16 committee is commendable and indeed necessary, but it will require close informal links with all active standards bodies throughout the world if conflicting practices are not to arise (already Western German standards DIN 19052 sheets 1 and 2 on engineering drawing systems—reviewed by K. Mieze (262)—specify some significant but possibly not incompatible reduction ratio requirements against those of BS 4210: Part 1).

A third source of British Standards may arise in future through the facilities to carry out original work within the United Kingdom at national centres such as the National Reprographic Centre for documentation (NRCd). Previous tendencies for BSI to rely exclusively on the adoption of standards produced elsewhere reflect the fact that BSI itself has only functioned as a secretariat and for ground-work has had to rely on committee members and the help of their employing organisations.

The Microfilm Association of Great Britain has a standards committee which took the initiative in microfiche standardisation in 1965 when it published a draft specification (263) based on American work which ultimately led to the publication of BS 4187. Paradoxically the importance of the committee's work was marked by the setting up of the BS PHC 16 committee and the participation of many MAOBG members directly in BSI work. Nevertheless, the MAOGB committee still exists to report back to members, and the association is formally represented on the BS PHC 16 committee.

Specific Microform Standards and Related Works

This section reviews existing British Standards and their relationship to overseas and other non-national standards.

BS 308: 1964 Supplement No. 1, 1967 (271)

This standard covers the preparation of drawings suitable for microfilming. It states that the practices recommended should involve no increases of man hours over those recommended in the main body of BS 308 on engineering drawings. Emphasis is placed on open layouts and the avoidance of cramped detail; minimum requirements for character size are specified as are line thicknesses and spacings. The standard related closely to BS 4210 (260) which specifies the overall system for the 35mm microcopying of engineering drawings. Unfortunately, there are some contradictions between the two standards. The two most obvious points of difference are represented by the illustration in BS 308 supplement of a non "A" sized drawing while BS 4210 is essentially based upon "A" sizes and the statement in BS 308 supplement 1 that drawings larger than "A1" will require sectionalising when in fact BS 4210 specifies sectionalising only above "AO" size.

British Standard 850-1955 (308)

A basic technical standard covering cinematographic 'safety film'. BS 1371 specifies that basic stock for microfilm should be in accordance with BS 850. BS 850 is primarily concerned with inflammability; it specifies a maximum nitrate content and a burning test.

British Standard 677—Parts 1 and 2: 1958 (272)

Another basic technical standard specifying the width and perforations of 16mm and 35mm microfilm and referenced in BS 1371 (125) as such.

British Standard 1193:1961 (273)

BS 1371 (125), which covers 70mm in addition to the more familiar 16mm and 35mm, specified that 70mm film shall conform in width and perforations to BS 1193.

British Standard 1153: 1955 (118)

Makes recommendations for the storage and processing of microfilm to two levels of permanence: "commercial" where a life of up to 25 years is required, and "archival" where the microforms are required for an indefinite lifetime. The removal of residual sodium thiosulphate (hypo) is an important element in archival permanence. This standard specifies the use of the Crabtree-Ross test (274) as a method of measurement for residual thiosulphate. The accuracy of the method has subsequently been questioned by C. I. Pope (275) of the National Bureau of Standards (U.S.A.). However, a careful balance has to be drawn between accuracy requirements and the need for a simple method suitable for use by non-scientific personnel. The standard method has also been criticised for its use of mercuric chloride in lethal quantities. In view of these two points the question of testing for residual thiosulphate is in need of a careful review. American Standard PH5.4 (124) is the American equivalent of BS 1153. According to P. Z. Adelstein (306) a proposed U.S.A. Standard to replace PH48: 1958 (276) includes some changes to the Crabtree-Ross test.

British Standard 1371: 1956 (125)

This standard covering microfilm readers and reels should be a corner-stone for roll film practice and equipment. Unfortunately, it has become considerably outdated in many respects—the requirements for 35mm readers, for example, have become outdated by the appearance of BS 4191: 1967 (278) while the dimensions for spools and reels are potentially outdated by the ISO draft recommendation 1528 dealing with 16mm spools and reels. The general practice of microrecording onto 16mm and 35mm dealt with in BS 1371 is also the subject of yet another ISO draft. It must be hoped that definitive ISO standards will appear in the near future to enable work to be put in hand on a revision of BS 1371. Meanwhile those responsible for general 35mm roll recording can look to the American Library Association's "Microfilm Norms" (127) for a good operational standard.

British Standard 4187: 1967 (5)

The British microfiche standard is based closely on the American Federal (or "COSATI") microfiche standard (64). Perhaps the main point of difference is the increase in the British Standard of the maximum reduction ratio from 1:20 to 1:22 to permit the recording of the obsolete but popular British foolscap size within the specified frame area. Since the "COSATI" standard was written around the requirements specifically of technical reports, it may be that ultimately a slightly more flexible British standard will be needed. J. L. Kish's report (307) that the new U.S. Standards Institute draft microfiche standard specifies pagination beginning at the lower rather than the upper left, as in the British Standard, demonstrates the problems of international co-ordination.

British Standard 4189: 1967 (258)

This is the first of the British Standards to be published relating to the ISO mire and micromire resolution test targets. It derives from ISO R 435 of an identical title (259). The standard specified the octagonal shape of the test character and explains the system of designation (mire characters are designated by their size in hundreths of millimetres, micromire characters by their size in thousandths of millimetres; in both cases in the series 50 63 80 100 125). Essentially the test characters are symbolic representations of typical characters of printed text and, therefore, in the case of the mire series, their use is based on the promise that, if a copying process can reproduce a given size of mire satisfactorily, it can be assumed that its same process will produce from a typeface of comparable size a legible result. Each octagon contains two diagonals which can be either vertical, horizontal, right inclined or left inclined. Characters are ranged into two "words" of characters randomly oriented. They are considered legible when the orientation of seven out of eight characters can be identified. The ability to identify mire characters in this way does not mean that the process could adequately render legible typefaces of the same size, since the test involves careful examination through a microscope and actual text which needed to be read in this way would hardly be accepted as legible in a practical sense. Nevertheless, if there is a relationship the standard has nothing to say on what it might be. In a similar manner the ten times smaller micro-mire can be used for assessing the resolution capabilities of readers. Unfortunately, neither the mire not the micro-mire are, as yet, obtainable from any certified agency either in Great Britain or elsewhere, and it has been generally impossible for any but theoretical projections of their usefulness to be made. During 1968 the National Reprographic Centre for documentation produced a trial batch of mires for assessment by BSI and commissioned the production of micro-mires by the National Cash Register Company using their PCMI process. Assessments so far indicate some doubts about the basic premise on which the mire character is based. It must be hoped that the matter will be resolved speedily since use of the mire target has already been specified in BS 4187. Fortunately, the readily available American National Bureau of Standards test targets provide a suitable and widely used, although unspecified (so far as BSI and ISO are concerned), alternative method.

British Standard 4191: 1967 (278)

This standard covering the essential characteristics of 35mm roll film readers is another ISO derived standard being based upon ISO Recommendation R 452. The use of the term "essential" in the title is fully justified since the standard specified precise requirements only for little more than image size and film lengths to be accommodated, the need for correct orientation of the image on the screen, the minimum magnification and temperature rise. The "general requirements" section of the standard provides a series of pointers which, since they are clearly a matter of individual interpretation, read strangely in a standard ("the apparatus shall be so designed as to permit unsupervised use, or use after brief instruction"). Other parts specify absolute standards which taken literally would be impossible to meet: "the use of the apparatus shall not cause such damage to the microfilm as to impair its future usefulness or legibility"—while it is possible to measure and therefore specify wear and tear factors (there is for example an American standard on the determination of scratch resistance (279)), they clearly cannot be eliminated entirely.

British Standard 4210 Part I: 1967 (260)

This standard covers the requirements for 35mm aperture card-based engineering drawings systems. Part I covers the overall system and specifies the range of original sizes, reduction ratios, enlargement ratios and similar topics. Parts 2 and 3 (as yet unpublished) will cover photographic requirements (background densities and resolution requirements) and aperture card specifications respectively.

The United States

It is surprising to find that the country which has produced two of the most important microform systems standards (on engineering drawing systems and microfiches) on which national standards in a large number of countries have been, or are being, based has not itself yet published the standards as American national standards. No doubt part of the answer may be found in the announcement in late 1966 (264) that a United States of America Standards Institute has been formed to replace the previous American Standards Association. It is possible that this announcement foretells the more rapid appearance of standards in the U.S.A. as actual, as opposed to virtual, national standards.

As it stands, however, the systems standards for aperture card-based engineering drawing systems which have clearly formed the basis for at least British and Western German standards (260 and 262) are published by the U.S. Department of Defense (DOD) as "Military" (MIL series) standards (261), and in fact critics of these standards have not been slow to point out their lack of national status. While each of the fifteen standards making up the total package relating to engineering drawing systems is separately obtainable from the DOD, users not concerned with the contractual basis of the standards will find the collected edition published by the National Microfilm Association (261) the most convenient package.

Likewise, the extremely significant A6 60 frame microfiche standard (64) originates from the U.S. Federal Council for Science and Technology Committee on Scientific and Technical Information, and is popularly referred to as the "COSATI" standard after the committee. Strictly, both of these standards are relevant only to U.S. Government departments and contractors.

The National Microfilm Association (NMA) in the U.S.A. has been active in the standards field for some time. From the NMA came the first microfiche standard which included in a range of alternative formats (75 x 125mm, 5 x 8 inches and 3.25 x 7.375 inches) the ubiquitous A6 sized 60 frame microfiche (168). In 1967 the original 1963 standard referred to above was replaced by a standard (69) which eliminated the 5 x 8 inch size, but which permitted, as an option, the use of higher reduction ratios (24:1 in addition to 20:1) to give a smaller frame size increasing the number of frame spaces on an A6 microfiche from 60 to 98. This standard is to be passed to the U.S. Standards Institute for consideration.

Earlier activities included the publication of an eight-page document specifying drafting techniques for drawings intended for microfilming by W. J. Gallagher and C. E. Nelson (265). As noted above, it performed a useful service in publishing a collected edition of the DOD MIL series of standards (261).

The NMA has an active committee TR-29.1 to make recommendations on standardisation for facsimile microform transmission (266). Following a mail survey the committee is initially concentrating on work in aperture card-based facsimile transmission systems.

The International Micrographic Congress (IMC) is a newer organisation which appears to exist primarily to promote international microform congresses outside the U.S.A. (Two have been held so far, in Tokyo and Frankfurt.) It has a standards committee under C. E. Nelson with representatives from twelve "major" countries. It proposes to bring together a consensus of opinion on standards and to present this to the International Standards Organisation to hasten the achievement of international standards; as part of this effort it intends to collect and disseminate national standards among members (267). Clearly an informal body of this type could carry out useful liaison activities complementary to the ponderous activities of ISO.

The National Bureau of Standards has done much useful research in support of the American Standards Association activities and will presumably continue in a similar relationship to the U.S. Standards Institute. Its work on archival quality and quality testing has been particularly significant. It does not itself now issue standards, but it is responsible for the widely used NBS resolution test charts. In the absence of any source of supply for the ISO mire test objects, the NBS test charts have attained international usage.

The American Library Association has produced in "Microfilm Norms" (127) a most valuable specification for the technical and bibliographical qualities of 35mm roll film for libraries. On the purely technical aspects it refers to U.S. Standards Institute (ex ASA) standards. It is reported to be considering a similar standard for microfiches.

Western Germany

The German standards organisation (Deutsche Normen) produces draft standards for the microrecording of engineering drawings in August 1967 (268). The standard overall differed substantially from the American MIL standards (261) and the British Standard (260) in that Part 1 permitted the use of 35mm, 70mm or 105mm roll film for inactive or archival recording of drawings. Part 2 is intended for microforms for external exchange or mechanical processing, and here the draft is akin to the British and American standards in that it specified the ubiquitous 35mm aperture card. Like the British Standard is assumes the use of originals of the international A series of sizes (for drawings AO to A5); it permits the use of either three reduction ratios (known as "part frame" since, with six sizes and only three ratios, image sizes do not necessarily utilise the complete frame area) or six ratios (known as "full frame" since each original size is matched to a ratio which utilises the full image area). Conversely, the British Standard caters for only five original sizes (AO to A4), and in permitting the option of full frame needs only an identical number of ratios, while it permits part frame on a three ratio basis as does the German standard. The final point of difference is that the German standard uses a different series of preferred number reduction ratios (1:29, 1:21, 1:148, 1:10.5, 1:7.4, 1:5.25) to the British Standard (1:30, 1:21.2, 1:15, 1.10.6, 1:7.5), but it may be that the ratios are sufficiently similar to avoid incompatibility. The American MIL standards, however, from which both the British and German work is derived, differs in that original paper sizes are in the American A to E series while the part frame only system uses the ratios 1:30, 1:24 and 1:16. (The technical factors underlying full and part frame recording are explained by B. J. S. Williams (59)).

The above demonstrates some of the problems of unilateral standardisation. However, differences between the German and British standards for active microforms are unlikely to result in incompatibility while, even given formal co-ordination via ISO, it is extremely doubtful if the Americans would have been persuaded to convert to the international "A" size papers which form the basis of the British and German standards for engineering drawings.

France

The French national standards organisation AFNOR have produced a microfiche standard (312) that differs very substantially from British and American microfiche standards (5 and 64). While it utilises the same external format (international A6 or 105 x 148mm), it permits the use of a very wide variety of frame sizes within the format (and to that extent could be said to pursue the European tradition noted by Hawken on page 27). It additionally allocates vertical strips on each edge of the microfiche, each 7.5mm wide, for the incorporation of retrieval codes. Horizontal title strips optionally 'petit' at 9.5mm or 'grand' at 21mm are specified. The remaining area for micro-images may then be divided in a specified manner into 1, 2, 4, 8, 12, 16, 32, 56 or 64 images giving a total range of frame size from a single 133 x 94.5 to below 16mm. Additionally, a non-homogenous fiche is permitted consisting of two combinations of frame sizes. This latter would permit, for example, eight frames of nominally 32 x 20mm and one of 65 x 95mm. Some examples of French microfiches show a fiche of this type used for a micro-image of an X-ray (in the large frame) and textual medical records (in the smaller frames). In another example a fiche of this type is used for the annual report of a railway company with a large frame used to show a railway scene. Since this is virtually eye legible, it represents an intriguing attempt to use graphics to improve the appearance and status of a microfiche in a similar way to which they would be used on the cover of a conventional document.

Ingenious as the concept of such flexible microfiches may be, it does pose some major questions on the likely cost of recording and, far more important, reading equipment able to cope adequately with such flexibility. The Centre de Documentation of the Centre National de la Recherche Scientifique, under J. J. Bastarde in Paris, has evolved an automatic camera for recording to this specification but there is no evidence of reader designs exhibiting the required flexibility.

APPENDIX 1

GLOSSARY OF TERMS USED IN THE TEXT

(Acknowledgements are due to the National Microfilm Association glossary of terms edited by D. M. Avedon (1) from which all of the terms marked with an asterisk are quoted unaltered.)

A

"A" sizes. An international series of paper sizes specified in British Standards. A6 is widely used and specified for microfiches.

Aperture Card*. A card with a rectangular hole or holes specifically designed to hold a frame or frames of microfilm.

Archival Quality* The degree to which a processed print or film will retain its characteristics during a period of use and storage. The ability to resist deterioration for a lengthy, specified time.

B

Back Projector Readers. Readers in which the enlarged image is projected onto the back of a translucent screen for reading from the front by transmitted light (contrast; front projectors).

Binary. A numbering system in which quantities are represented in base 2 rather than base 10. Binary digits (bits) may be optically recorded as opaque and transparent areas of film.

Book Holder. A device which permits the rapid photographing of large bound books. The carriage has balanced or spring-loaded platens so that two pages may be photographed at a time.

C

Camera* A photographic device, employing an optical system, used for exposing light-sensitive material.

Camera, Microfiche. See Camera, step-and-repeat.

Camera, Planetary (Flat-Bed)* A type of microfilm camera in which the document being photographed and the film remain in a stationary position during the exposure. The document is on a plane surface at time of filming.

Camera, Rotary (Flow)* A type of microfilm camera that photographs documents while they are being moved by some form of transport mechanism. The document transport mechanism is connected to a film transport mechanism, and the film also moves during exposure so that there is no relative movement between the film and the image of the document.

Camera, Step-and-Repeat* A type of microfilm camera which can expose a series of separate images on an area of film according to a predetermined format, usually in orderly rows and columns.

Cassette. A container for processed roll microfilm which facilitates rapid insertion into a reader or reader/printer and which eliminates the need for hand threading of the film.

Cathode Ray Tube Recorder. A microfilm camera recording from a cathode ray tube display; the two normally form an integral unit. Typically the display is generated from computer produced magnetic tape and the unit thus provides a facility for direct microform computer output.

Coupler* In a diazo material the coupler is a compound which combines with the unexposed diazonium salt to form the visible dye image.

Curl* Departure from physical flatness in the length of film or paper. To tend to roll up. (See Bow.) (See also ASA PH 1.29.)

D

Densitometer* An instrument used to measure optical density. Two basic types exist:

1 Transmission—used to measure the opacity of film images.
2 Reflection—used to measure the amount of light reflected by a surface.

Density* The light-absorbing quality of a photographic image (degree of opacity of film and blackness for prints, usually expressed as the logarithm of the opacity). Several specific types of density values for a photograph may be expressed but diffuse transmission density is the one of greatest use in the case of microfilm and diffuse reflection density is generally of interest for prints. See U.S.A. Standards PH 2.17 and PH 2.19.

Desk Top Libraries. Packaged libraries published on microforms (see Packaged Libraries).

Diazo Material* A slow print film or paper, sensitized by means of diazonium salts which, subsequent to exposure to light strong in the blue to ultra-violet spectrum and development, forms an image. Diazo material generally produces non-reversible images, i.e., a positive image will produce a positive image and a negative image will produce a negative image.

E

Emulsion* A photographic material coating in which light-sensitive materials are suspended such as silver halides.

Enlarger-Printer* A machine which projects an enlarged image from microfilm, develops, and fixes the image on a suitable material.

F

File Integrity. The integrity of a file depends upon the degree to which its contents are complete and in correct sequence. Roll microfilm demonstrates good file integrity since once recorded individual items cannot normally become disordered or lost.

Film Frame* The area of film exposed to light through the camera optical system during one exposure, regardless of whether or not the area is filled by the document image.

Fixing* The part of photographic processing which dissolves the undeveloped silver halides from a processed film or print to render the developed image more permanent.

Format, external. The form (flat or roll) and external dimensions of a microform.

Format, internal. The internal arrangement of microforms variables are the orientation, arrangement, sequence and size of images.

Frame, Microfiche*

1 One micro-image and margin contained within a film frame.

2 A single area of a grid pattern.

Frame Size* The dimensions of the film frame.

Front Projector Readers (external projectors). Readers in which the enlarged image is projected onto the front of an opaque screen and read by reflected light (contrast back projectors).

Frost Xerography. An unconventional recording process combining xerographic and thermoplastic techniques.

G

Generation* A measure of the remoteness of the copy from the original document. The picture taken of the document is termed "first generation" microfilm (camera microfilm). Copies made from this "first generation" are termed "second generation" and copies from the "second generation" are termed "third generation", etc. First and third generation are known as odd, and second and fourth generations are even.

H

Hard Copy* An enlarged copy usually on paper.

Hardener* A chemical which increases the melting point of gelatin in photographic layers and prevents softening in warm processing baths. Hardeners commonly used in photographic processing baths are: aluminium potassium sulphate, and formaldehyde solution.

I

Image* A representation of an object or information produced by means of light rays.

K

Kalvar* A trademark for the film and equipment products of the Kalvar Corporation. See also Vesicular Film.

M

Magnetic Tape. A length of film on which there is a coating generally of iron oxide particles held in a binder across which information can be recorded in magnetic tracks.

Master Film* Any film, but generally a negative, which is used for producing further reproductions.

Master Negative* See Master Film.

Microcard* A trademark of the Microcard Corporation for a micro-opaque card.

Microfiche* A sheet of microfilm containing multiple micro images in a grid pattern. It usually contains a title which can be read without magnification.

Microfilm*

1 A fine-grain, high resolution film containing an image greatly reduced in size from the original.

2 The recording of micro-photographs on film.

3 Raw film with characteristics as in 1.

Microform* A generic term for any form, either film or paper, which contains micro-images.

Micro-Image* A unit of information, such as a page of text or a drawing too small to be read without magnification.

Micro-Opaques* A sheet of opaque material bearing one or more micro-images.

Microprint, Readex* A trademark of Readex Microprint Corporation for a micro-opaque card produced by a printing press process using ink on paper. (See Micro-Opaque.)

Mire. The resolution test target specified in ISO recommendations. (See Resolution in glossary. Targets, resolution test in subject index.)

N

Negative* A photographic image with light lines, characters, and tones on a dark background.

O

Original Micropublication. The publication of material on microform only, or its publication on microform prior to or simultaneously with the full-sized publication. (See Retrospective Micropublication.)

P

Packaged Libraries. Material collected by subject or form and republished, generally on microforms, as a complete library including subject, author and other indexes and regular updating.

PCMI* A trademark of the National Cash Register Company. Photo-Chromic Micro Image is a photographic technique for information recording at very high reductions developed by the National Cash Register Company.

Photo-Chromic* See PCMI.

Positive* A photographic image with dark lines, characters, and tones on a light background.

Print-out. An enlarged print made from a micro-image.

R

Reader* A projection device for viewing an enlarged micro-image with the unaided eye.

Reader/printer* A machine which combines the functions of a reader and an enlarger-printer.

Reduction Ratio. The ratio of the linear measurement of a document to the linear measurement of the image of the same document expressed as 16:1, 20:1, etc.

Resolution. The ability of optical systems and photo-materials to render visible fine detail of an object; a measure of sharpness of an image, expressed as the number of lines per millimetre, discernible in an image. Resolution in processed microfilm is a function of film emulsion, exposure, camera lens, camera adjustment, camera vibration, and film processing. Resolution is measured by examining a micro-filmed resolution test chart under a microscope to determine the smallest pattern in which lines can be distinguished both horizontally and vertically.

Retrospective Micropublication. The re-issue in microformat of material some time after full-sized publication (see also Original Micropublication).

Roll Microfilm* A length of microfilm on a reel, spool or in a cassette.

S

Screen* A surface onto which an image is projected.

Shelf Life* The period of time before deterioration renders a material unusable.

Sign Reversal. In sign-reversing photographic systems the sign changes when a further generation is produced; negatives reproduce as positives and vice versa.

Silver Halide* A compound of silver and one of the following elements known as halogens: fluorine, chlorine, bromide and iodine.

Splice. A joint made between two pieces of film so that they function as a single piece.

T

Targe*

1 Any document or chart containing identification information, coding or test charts.

2 An aid to technical or bibliographic control which is photographed on the film preceding or following the document. (Microfilm Norms, ALA.)

Thermoplastic Recording. Thermoplastic recording entails the use of substances which become soft and pliable when heated and which retain their shape on cooling. In unconventional microrecording processes, a micro-image written or recorded onto a thermoplastic layer is created by the deformation of the material on cooling.

Track. A path along which information is recorded on magnetic tape.

U

Ultra High Reduction Ratios. Reduction ratios exceeding 1:100.

Unitize*

1 The separation of a roll of microfilm into individual frames and their insertion in a carrier.

2 To microfilm on one or more sheets of microfiche a unit of information, such as a report, a specification or a periodical.

V

Vesicular Film* Film which has the light-sensitive element suspended in a plastic layer and which upon exposure creates strains within the layer in the form of a latent image. The strains are released and the latent image made visual by heating the plastic layer. The image becomes permanent when the layer cools.

X

Xerography (Electrostatic)* A generic term for the formation of a latent electrostatic image by action of light on a photoconducting insulating surface. The latent image may be made visual by a number of methods such as applying charged pigmented powders which are attracted to the latent image. The powder particles either directly or by transfer may be applied and fixed to a suitable medium. See Webster's Unabridged Dictionary, Third Edition.

APPENDIX 2 : **List of Sources**

Serial No.	*Reference*
1	Avedon, D. M. (editor): Glossary of terms for micro-photography and reproductions made from micro-images, 4th edition.
2	Luther, F., Language of Lilliput: a thesaurus for users of microfilm Parts 1–7. Library Journal, Vol. 86, pp 929-932, 2425-2430, 3238-3241, 3743-3746. Vol. 87, pp 48-54, 920-931.
3	International Organisation for Standardisation. ISO recommendation R 371: 1964—Terminology of microcopy apparatus.
4	International Organisation for Standardisation. ISO recommendation R 260: 1962—terms relating to microcopies and their bases. 4 pages.
5	British Standards Institution. BS 4187: 1967. Specification for microfiches.
6	Ballou, H. W.: Microfilm topics; micro-semantics. Systems Management, October 1961.
7	Crow, J. E.: Microreproductions and technical information. NMA Proceedings, 13th annual meeting and convention, 1964. Proceedings, pp 89-97. NMA, 1964
8	Avedon, D. M.: Why do we need a Glossary of Microfilm Terms? NMA Proceedings, 11th annual meeting and convention 1962, pp 345-348.
9	Borden, F. R.: New DOD specifications for microfilming; a panel. NMA Proceedings, 12th annual meeting and convention 1963, pp 82-90.
10	Howerton, P. W.: The Case for Realism in Document Storage Systems. NMA Proceedings, 11th annual meeting and convention 1962, pp 21-25.
11	Hawkins, R.: Production of Microforms. Rutgers State University, 1960. (State of the library art series, Vol. 5, Part 1.)
12	Steward, J., Hickey, D. and others: Reading devices for micro-images. Rutgers State University, 1960. (State of the library art series, Vol. 5, Pt. 2).
13	Luther, F.: Microfilm, a history 1839-1900. NMA 1959.
14	Browning, W.: John Benjamin Dancer, F.R.R.A.S., 1812-1887. An autobiographical sketch with some letters. Manchester Literary and Philosophical Society, 1965.
15	Pollard, A. F. C.: Miniature and Microscopic Documents. The proceedings of the British Society for International bibliography. 29th Ordinary Meeting, 28th September, 1943, Vol. 5, Pt. 3, pp 43-54.
16	Ballou, H. W.: Copying methods notes; microform picture windows. Library Resources, Vol. 8, Pt. 4, Fall 1964, pp 449-455.
17	Seidel, A.: The photomicrographic reproduction of documents. Science Vol. 80, 24th August, 1934, pp 184-185.
18	Goebel, J.: Erfindung der Plantilus-Mikrokopie (The invention of the flat microfiche-sheet). Bueromarkt 1965, Pt. 25, pp 17-20, Pt. 26, pp 29-30, 1966 Pt. 1, pp 27-31, Pt. 2, pp 19-22.
19	Taubes, E. P.: The Use of Microfilm as a Systems Tool. Internationaler Kongress fuer Reprographie, Cologne, 14-19th October, 1963. Papers edited by O. Helwich (published as "Reprographie") Darmstadt, Helwich, 1964, pp 36-43.
20	Voskresenski, J.: The 75 x 125mm microfiche for multiple images. 1st Internationaler Kongress fuer Reprographie, Cologne, 14-19th October, 1963. Papers edited by O. Helwich. Darmstadt, Helwich, 1964, pp 334-335. (Published as "Reprographie").
21	De Sola, R.: Microfilming. New York, Essential Books, 1944.
22	Yerkes, C. P.: Microforum—microfilms used in cameras. Plan and Print, Vol. N40, Pt. 12, December, 1967, pp 12-13.
23	Hawken, W. R.: Copying methods manual. American Library Association, 1968 (LTP Publication No. 11).
24	Henn, R. W., and Wiest, D. G.: Microscopic spots: a progress report. NMA Proceedings, annual meeting and convention, 1964. pp 99-107.
25	National Bureau of Standards. Inspection of processed photographic record films for aging blemished, by C. S. McCamy, U.S. Department of Commerce, N.B.S. (N.B.S. handbook 96).
26	Pope, C. I.: Stability of residual thiosulphate in processed microfilm. Journal of Research of the National Bureau of Standards, Vol. 67C, Pt. 1, January-March, 1963, pp 15-24.
27	McCamy, C. S., and Pope, C. I.: Current Research on preservation of archival records on silver-gelatin type microfilm in roll form. Journal of Research of the National Bureau of Standards, Vol. 69A, September, 1965, pp 385-395.
28	Peiz, G. T.: Film coatings—do they really protect microfilm? National Micro-News, Pt. 67, December, 1963, pp 125-139.
29	Henn, R. W., and Mack, B. D.: "A gold protective treatment for microfilm" Photography, Science and Engineering, Vol. 9, Pt. 6, November-December, 1965, pp 378-384.

30 Fromm, H. J., and Insalaco, S. C.: "A new direct duplication silver halide film". National Micronews, Pt. 83, 1966, pp 3-13.

31 Eastman Kodak Co.: New Recordak Direct Duplicating films introduced at NMA National Convention. (Press Release).

32 Axford, A. J. O.: "Introductory Address" (Processes other than silver halide and electrophotographic). 1st Internationaler Kongress fuer Reprographie, Cologne, 14-19th October, 1963. Papers edited by O. Helwich (published as "Reprographie") Darmstadt, Helwich, 1964, pp 167-171.

33 Benbrook, C. H.: Diazo-type duplication of microfilm. Photographic Eng. Vol. 7, Pt. 1, 1956, pp 7-11.

34 Smith, G. W. Characteristics of diazo film microfilm duplicates. Journal of Photographic Science, March/April, 1962, pp 83-91.

35 Boone, J. W., and Todd, H. S.: "Considerations in Selecting Diazo film for Image Storage and Retrieval Systems", NMA Proceedings, 12th annual meeting and convention, 1963, pp 137-148.

36 Deley, J. P., and Dyer, J. S.: A Review of Federal Specifications L-F-315b. NMA Journal, 1(2), Winter, 1968, pp 49-52.

37 Kasik, B. R.: "The High Production Manufacture of Duplicate Microfilm", NMA Proceedings, 11th annual meeting and convention, 1962, pp 123-136.

38 Q's and A's about Diazo. Systems, Vol. 7, Pt. 6, June, 1966, pp 16, 17 and 36.

39 National Reprographic Centre for documentation. TER 67/2 Evaluation of the Atlantic F66 microfiche reader. November 1967, 29 pages.

40 Scott, P.: "Brief Survey of Materials for Image Storage", NMA Proceedings, 12th annual meeting and convention, 1963, pp 93-104.

41 Dugan, J. M., Feichtinger, H. I. G., and Walkup, L. E.: "Imaging Media for Information Storage and Retrieval Systems", NMA Proceedings, 12th annual meeting and convention, 1963, pp 127-136.

42 Sandlin, E. E., and Anderson, M. G.: Vesicular Systems for High Resolution Generation Printing. NMA Proceedings, 13th annual meeting and convention, 1964, pp 189-199.

43 Rabedeau, M. E.: "The Micro-Image Characteristics of a Kalvar Film". Photographic Science and Engineering, Pt. 1, pp 58-62.

44 Nieset, R. T.: Theory and Control of Light Scattering as applied in the Kalvar Process. 1st Internationaler Kongress fuer Reprographie, Cologne, 14-19th October, 1963. Papers edited by O. Helwich (published as "Reprographie"). Darmstadt, Helwich, 1964, pp 177-180.

45 Caps Consultants Ltd.: "Kalvar Photographic Materials", 1963, 19 pages. (Microreproduction 4.)

46 Duplicating Microfilm. Reproduction, Vol. 3, Pt. 10, October, 1966, pp 37-39.

47 Wilson, T.: Application of ultraviolet optics to printing processes. National Microfilm Association Proceedings, 13th annual meeting and convention, 1964, pp 79-87.

48 Lindquist, R. M., and Rabedeau, M. E.: "Instrumentation for Standardised Testing of Kalvar Films", NMA Proceedings, 12th annual meeting and convention, 1963, pp 149-160.

49 Goodwald, J. P.: Storage and reproduction of mapping data. NMA Journal, Vol. 1, No. 3, Spring 1968, pp 82-84.

50 Kalvar camera-developer announced. National Micro-News, Pt. 76, June 1965, pp 243-245.

51 —

52 Levinthal, J. G.: Thermoplastic Film Recording; a new technique for microreproduction. NMA Proceedings, 12th annual meeting and convention, 1963, pp 119-125.

53 Sharp and Oughton: The Micrographic information systems market in the U.S.A., 2 volumes, Chicago, Sharp & Oughton, 1965.

54 Gundlach, R. W.: Xerographic Frost Imaging. 1st Internationaler Kongress fuer Reprographie, Cologne, 14-19th October, 1963, papers edited by O. Helwich (published as "Reprographie"), Darmstadt, Helwich, 1964, pp 161-166.

55 Claus, C. J., and Sullivan, W. A.: Micro-images by Frost Xerography. Reprographics, Vol. 4, Pt. 10, November 1966, pp 21-23, 36.

56 Verry, H. R., and Wright, C. H.: Microcopying methods, London, Focal Press, 1967.

57 Kish, J. L.: Microfilm in business, New York, Ronald Press, 1966.

58 Baker, G. C.: The different forms of microfilm. Business Systems and Equipment, December 1967, pp 15, 18, 20 and 23.

59 Williams, B. J. S.: Evaluation of microrecording techniques for information and data storage and retrieval, Hatfield, Hertis, 1967.

60 Tate, V. D.: An appraisal of microfilm. American Documentation, Vol. 1, 1950, pp 91-99.

61 Scott, P.: Advances and goals in microphotography. Library Trends, Vol. 8, 1960, pp 458-492.

62 Dickison, R. R.: The Scholar and the Future of Microfilm. American Documentation, Vol. 17, Pt. 4, October 1966, pp 178-179.

63 Rider, F.: The Scholar and the Future of the Research Library. New York, Hadhan Press, 1944.

64 U.S.A. Federal Council for Science and Technology Committee on Scientific and Technical Information (COSATI). Federal microfiche standards. Office of Science and Technology, September 1965, 14 pages.

65 Special Libraries Association, Government Information Services Committee Users' look at information centers, Special libraries, Vol. 57, 1966, pp 45-50.

66 Williams, B. J. S., and Wright, G. H.: Microforms, an active tool for library systems. Microdoc, Vol. 6, Pt. 1, 1967, pp 3-14.

67 Heilprin, L. B.: The Economics of 'On Demand' Library Copying. NMA Proceedings, 11th annual meeting and convention, 1962, pp 311-339.

68 Hawken, W. R.: Microform standardisations, the problem of research materials and a proposed solution, NMA Journal, Vol. 2, No. 1, Fall 1968, pp 14-27.

69 NMA M-1-1967. Microfiche standard specification, National Micro-News, No. 85, 1966, pp 81-98.

70 Williams, G.: The preservation of deteriorating books, Part 1, an examination of the problem. Library Journal, Vol. 91, Pt. 1, January 1966.

71 Williams, B. J. S.: Microforms in the U.S.A. 1966. Hatfield College of Technology, 1967. 48 pages.

72 Visit to the Royal Library, The Hague, Holland. Hatfield College of Technology. DES/Hertis Field Survey Reports 46 and 47 (unpublished).

73 Babiczky, B.: Az Orszagos Szechenyi konyvtar mikrofilmtara (The Microfilm Service of the National Szechenyi Library). Budapest, Evkonye 1960, pp 38-53. English summary pp 343-345.

74 Jackson, W. A.: Some limitations of microfilm. Papers of the Bibliographical Society of America, Vol. 35, 4th quarter 1941, pp 281-288.

75 University of London Library. Photocopying services (pamphlet), 4 pages, 1965.

76 Microcard Editions Inc., Catalog of publications, 1963.

77 Microcard Editions Inc. Microcard/Microfiche catalog 1964.

78 Microcard Editions Inc. Guide to microforms in print. Annually, 1961.

79 Microcard Editions Inc. Microcard/microfiche catalog, 1959.

80 Micro Methods Ltd., Field Survey Report No. 12, 1966 (Hatfield College of Technology, DES/Hertis research project. Unpublished).

81 Micro Methods Ltd., Catalogue (irregular).

82 Micromethods Ltd., Theses in microform (irregular).

83 Aslib Index to theses accepted for higher degrees in the universities of Great Britain and Ireland, Vol. 1, 1950/51 onwards.

84 Readex Microprint Corporation (U.K.) Ltd. Readex Microprint publications (as issued).

85 Research Publications NV., Leiden, Holland: Field Survey Report 45 (Hatfield College of Technology DES/Hertis research project. Unpublished).

86 University Microfilms Ltd., and Rank Xerox Copy Services. Field Survey Report No. 15 (Hatfield College of Technology DES/Hertis research project. Unpublished).

87 University Microfilms Ltd.: Modern periodicals on microfilm (irregular).

88 Tilton, E. M.: A union list of publications in opaque microforms. New York, Scarecrow Press, 2nd ed., 1964.

89 Liste de revues et collections de science humaines reproduites sous form de microfilms, microfiches "microcards" et "reprints". (List of periodicals and collections on human sciences reproduced in the form of microfilms, microfiches, micro-opaques and reprints). Maison des Sciences de L'homme, Services Bibliotheque-Documentation, 131 boulevard Saint Michel, Paris 5e. 2 Vols., 1965.

90 Microtexts as Media for Publication. A symposium held at Hatfield Technical College, 10th November, 1959. Programme, synopsis and list of delegates. Hatfield College of Technology, Hertis, 1959.

91 The cost-saving aspects of microfilming. The Office Machine Guide, Pt. 54, April, 1967, pp 25-31.

92 Clapp, V. W., and Jordan, R. T.: Re-evaluation of Microfilm as a Method of Book Storage. College and Research Libraries. Vol. 24, Pt. 1, January 1963, pp 5-15.

93 Pritzker, A. B., and Sadler, J. W.: An evaluation of microfilm as a method of book storage. College and Research Libraries, Vol. 18, July 1957, pp 290-296.

94 Use of Microfilm for Periodical Storage. UNESCO bulletin for libraries, Vol. 11, 1957, pp 53-56.

95 The Economist, 1966, 13th August, pp 629.

96 Power, E. B.: O-P books; a library breakthrough. American Documentation, Vol. 4, Pt. 4, 1958, pp 273-276.

97 Aldern, J.: Reproduction vs. preservation; a re-appraisal of the trend towards indiscriminate photo reproduction of rare books and manuscripts. Library Journal 1 November 1966, pp 5319-5322.

98 National Bureau of Standards. Inspection of processed photographic record films for aging and blemishes by C. S. McCamy. NBS handbook 96. U.S. Department of Commerce, N.B.S. 1964, 11 pages.

99 University Microfilms. World's First National Library of Enlarged Books for partially sighted readers, March 1966, 4 pages.

100 Hawken, W. R.: Microforms 1967 in Libraries, archives and educational institutions. Microfiche Foundation Newsletter, No. 15, August 1967, pp 3-8.

101 Veaner, A. B.: High Speed Reproduction of Library Cards through Micro-reproduction Techniques, NMA Proceedings, 13th annual meeting and convention, 1964, pp 159-163.

102 Loud, R. W.: Microfilm uses and products for libraries. Bay State Librarian, vol. 56, April, 1966, pp 7-18.

103 Kozumplik, W. A., and Lange, R. T.: Computer-produced microfilm library catalog. American Documentation, 1967, Vol. 18, Pt. 2, April, pp 67-80.

104 Bibliotheque Nationale, Bibliographical Control of Microcopies. UNESCO bulletin for Libraries, Vol. 19, May 1965, pp 136-160.

105 The Library of Congress. National Register of Microform Masters. Scientific Information Notes, April/May 1965, pp 2-3.

106 Library of Congress to house National Register of microfilms. Publishers Weekly, Vol. 187, pp 137-138, 1965.

107 Applebaum, E. L.: Implications of the National Register of Microform Masters as a part of a national preservation program. Library Resources and Technical Services. Vol. 9, Pt. 4, Fall 1965, pp 489-494.

108 Register of Microform Masters to be set up at the Library of Congress. Library Journal, Vol. 90, Pt. 15, March 1965, pp 1280-1281.

109 Microfilm Association of Great Britain. Copyright sub-committee. Report on legal deposit in relation to microtexts. 1968, 4 pages (Unpublished).

110 Pickford, A. G. A.: Fair (Fast access information retrieval) Project; Aims and Methods. Aslib Proceedings, Vol. 19, No. 3, pp 79-95.

111 Wright, G. H.: The Programme of the National Reprographic Centre for documentation. Institute of Reprographic Technology Symposium at the Repro-exhibition, London, 12-17 March 1967, pp 85-89.

112 Simonton, W.: Library Handling of Microforms. NMA Proceedings, 11th annual meeting and convention 1962, pp 277-282.

113 Saxena, T. P., and Saifuddin, M. A. H.: The Problems of Cataloguing Microforms. Aligarh Muslim Univ. Library, Science Dept., 1961, 14 pages, bibliography.

114 Eckles, R. B.: Some problems in scholarly uses of Microphoto publication. American Archivist, Vol. 17, 1964, pp 565-567.

115 American Historical Association. Guide to photocopies historical materials in the United States and Canada.

116 U.S.A. Library of Congress. National Register of Microform Masters No. 1 (September 1965) onwards.

117 Weber, D. C.: Design of a microtext reading room. UNESCO Bulletin for Libraries, Vol. 20, Pt. 6, November/December 1966, pp 303-308.

118 British Standards Institution, B.S. 1153: 1955. Recommendations for the storage of microfilm.

119 Scott, C. F.: The microforms reading room at the University of London Library. Microdoc, Vol. 6, Pt. 3, 1967, pp 65-67.

120 Veaner, A. B.: A proposed Shop Manual for Library Reproduction Services. NMA Proceedings, 12th annual meeting and convention, 1963, pp 207-215.

121 Library of Congress. Specifications for Library of Congress microfilming by S. R. Salmon, 1964, 21 pages.

122 American Standard Association. PH 13.1-1958. Method for determining the brittleness of photographic film.

123 American Standards Association. PH1.28-1957. American standard specifications for photographic films for permanent records. 11 pages.

Serial No.	*Reference*
124	American Standards Association. PH5.4-1957. American standard practice for storage of microfilm, 11 pages.
125	British Standards Institution. BS 1371: 1956. Microfilm readers and reels, 15 pages.
126	Holmes, D. C.: Quality Control at the Library of Congress. NMA Proceedings, 13th annual convention and meeting, 1964, pp 207-217.
127	American Library Association. Resources and Technical Services Division. Microfilm Norms; Recommended standards for libraries prepared by the library standards for Microfilm Committee of the copying methods section, Resources and Technical Services Division. American Library Association. 1966, 48 pages.
128	U.K. Ministry of Technology; Warren Spring Laboratory. Purchasing specification for microfiches, by P. S. Harris. Warren Spring Laboratory 1969, 8 pages (SBN 900790 27X).
129	U.S. National Bureau of Standards. Report 9446. A study of the requirements and specifications for serial and monograph microrecording for the National Library of Medicine, by E. J. Forbes and T. C. Bagg. U.S. Department of Commerce, 1966, 100 pages.
130	National Microfilm Association, Standards Committee. Proposal to revise NMA Microfiche Standards Specification M-1-1963. National Micro News No. 78. October 1965, pp 58-69.
131	UNESCO. Survey of Microfilm Use. 43 pages. 1951 (reprint from paper by J. J. Bastardie, UNESCO Bulletin for Libraries, Vol. 6, Pts. 2 and 3, Feb./March, 1952 and Pts. 5 and 6, May/June 1952.
132	The ISO mire and micromire. NRCd bulletin, February 1968, pp 1-4.
133	Hawken, W. R.: Enlarged prints from library microforms. American Library Association, 1961, 131 pages.
134	American Library Association, Library Technology Project, Annual Reports 1965-66, 7 pages.
137	Piez, G. T.: Library Technology Project: A world-wide service. Unesco Bulletin for Libraries, Vol. 19, Pt. 5, Sept.-Oct., 1965, pp 232-236.
138	Piez, G. T.: Library Technology Project; past, present and projected future. Library Quarterly, Vol. 35, Pt. 2, April, 1965, pp 97-108.
139	Heilprin, L. B.: Communication Engineering Approach to Microforms. NMA Proceedings, 10th annual meeting and convention, April 1961, pp 80-92.
140	Scott, P.: Project Intrex and Microphotography; Appendix K to Intrex. Report of a Planning Conference on Information Transfer Experiments, 3rd Sept. 1965, edited by C. F. J. Overhage and R. J. Harman, 1965, pp 203-214, Massachusettes Institute of Technology Press.
141	Alexander, S. N., and Rose, F. C.: Current Status of Graphic Storage Techniques; their potential application to library mechanisation; with Appendix, facsimile storage and retrieval system descriptions. (In conference on libraries and automation.) Airlie Foundation 1963. Library of Congress 1964, pp 11-40.
142	Diaz A.: Microreproduction information sources. Library resources and Technical services, Spring 1967, pp 211-214.
143	Union List of Microfilms. (First published in 1942 by the Philadelphia Bibliographic Center and Union Library Catalogue. Supplements 1-5 appeared 1943-47. In 1951 a cumulated edition was published—Union list of microfilms, revised, enlarged and cumulative edition—followed by supplements 1949-52 and 1952-55. A final accumulation was published by Edward Brothers in 1961.)
144	Library of Congress. Newspapers on microfilm, 305 pages, 1948.
145	Council on Library Resources. $63,000 for development of Microfiche Equipment. TM-C Report on Microfiche, Vol. 1, No. 4, October 1965, pp 2.
146	Hailey, F.: In sight of the "no-paper" office. Business Systems and Equipment, August 1967, pp 21-22
147	U.S. Patent Office. All patents since 1790 are going on to microfilm. New York Times, Friday, 1 July 1966.
148	U.S. Patent Office. All U.S. patents issued 1790 to be microfilmed. National Micronews, No. 83, 1966, pp 30-32.
149	U.S. Patent Office. All U.S. patents to be microfilmed by mid-1968. Modern office procedures, Vol. 11, Pt. 11, November 1966, pp 42.
150	Mueller-Saala, H.: Microfilm in the Patent Service. ("Mikrofilm im Patent-dienst".). Reprographie Pt. 7, 1967, pp 185-188. (In German.)
151	Thomas Publishing Co., Trade literature on the Thomas Micro Catalogue Service, 1966.
152	Information Handling Services Inc. V.S.M.F. (Visual Search Microfilm File). Trade literature, 1965.
153	Information Handling Inc. Product microfiles go international. Product Engineering, Vol. 37, 23 May 1966, pp 91.

154 Technical Information on Microfilm Ltd. Desk for information service for engineers (product literature), 6 pages, February 1968.

155 Rank Organisation Ltd. Microfilm in U.K. Libraries, April 1964, 17 pp.

156 Microfiche Foundation. Various Applications of the Microfiche. Based on a paper read by Dr. L. J. Van Der Wolk, at the International Congress on Documentation and Information in Science and Industry, Rome 2-11 February, 1964. Delft. Microfiche Foundation, 12 pages, 1965 (Publications on the microfiche number 13).

157 Microfiche Foundation. Studying with microfiche. Delft, Microfiche Foundation, 1964. (Publications on the microfiche number 1.)

158 Wright, G. H.: Microrecording in the U.S.A., 1965. Hatfield College of Technology, 1965, 22 pages.

159 Bixby, W. E.: Applications of Microxerographic Techniques to Information Recording. NMA Proceedings, 11th annual meeting and convention, 1962, pp 229-247.

160 CLR orders development of a Filmcard Camera-Processor. Scientific Information Notes, Aug./Sept. 1965, pp 15-16.

161 Houston Fearless Corporation. The "CARD" system n.d. (Oct. 1967), 100 pages (approximately).

162 Jordan, R. T.: The complete package College Library. College and Research Libraries, September 1962, pp 405-409, 421.

163 —

164 Tauber, A. S., and Myers, W. C.: Photochromic Micro-images; A key to practical micro-document storage and dissemination. NMA Proceedings, 11th annual meeting and convention 1962, pp 257-269.

165 Desmond, A.: Microfilming at the British Museum. Industrial and Commercial Photographer, Vol. 8, Pt. 3, March 1968, pp 67-71.

166 Kleukens, C. H., and Goebel, J.: Schrift letter microkopie. (Handwriting, type, microcopy.) Mainzer Presse, Mainz 1940, 25 pages (Microfiche).

167 Van Der Wolk, L. J.: Publishing on Microfiche. Microtexts as media for publication; the papers and discussions of a symposium held at Hatfield College of Technology on 10th November 1959, Hertis 1960, pp 27-41.

168 National Microfilm Association. M-1-1963 Microfiche standard specification for documents $8\frac{1}{2}$ x 11 inches and smaller. National Micro-News, Pt. 66, October 1963, pp 42-52.

169 Baptie, A. L.: The New Publishing Prodigy—Microfiche. NMA Proceedings, 13th annual meeting and convention, 1964, pp 257-263.

170 Deighton, L. C.: The future of printing in a data-hungry society. Publishers Weekly, Vol. 189, Pt. 5, 31 January 1966, pp 55-60.

171 Hattery, L. H.: Microfiche comes of age as a publishing medium. Book Production Industry, Vol. 42, Pt. 12, December 1966, pp 46-49.

172 Tauber, A. S.: The Dynamic Use of Microfiche. NMA Proceedings 15th annual meeting and convention 1966, offprint, 15 pages.

173 Herbert, P.: Microfiche moves in. Business Systems and Equipment, November 1967, pp 27 and 29.

174 Rice, S.: Publishing in the Microforms. NMA Proceedings 11th annual meeting and convention 1962, pp 271-276.

175 Micropublications International. Microfiche preprints to be issued by New Gordon and Breach subsidiary. Scientific Information Notes, Vol. 9, No. 1, Feb./March 1967, pp 30-31.

176 Micropublications International Division of Gordon and Breach, Science Publishers Inc. 150 5th Avenue, New York N.Y. 10011. Microfiche publications program (promotion literature), no date.

177 U.S. Food and Drug Administration "Publications on Microfiche". Microfiche Foundation Newsletter, No. 13, January 1967, page 20.

178 Herman, C. M., and Davis, D. E.: Primary publication in microprint; a progress report on an experiment to demonstrate practicality of such a publication. Bio Science, Vol. 14, Pt. 4, April 1964, pp 27-30.

179 The International Microfilm Journal of Legal Medicine, 520 First Avenue, New York, N.Y. 10016, U.S.A. Publicity literature.

180 Chemical Abstracts on microfilm (promotional literature). American Chemical Society.

181 Weil, V. H., Emerson, W. G., Bolles, S. W., Lewenz, G. F.: Journal of Chemical Documentation, Vol. 5, Pt. 4, November 1965, pp 193-200.

182 Speekenbrink, J.: The use of Flat-Films Microcopy within the Framework of a Medical Abstracting Journal. Internationaler Kongress fur Reprographie 1st, Kologne 14-19th October 1963. Papers edited by O. Helwich (published as "Reprographie"), Darmstadt. Helwich, 1964, pp 351-352.

Serial No.	*Reference*
183	Day, M. S.: The NASA Microform Concept. NMA Proceedings, 13th annual meeting and convention 1964, pp 279-285.
184	Baptie, A. L.: Microfiche and research reports. National Micro-News, Pt. 74, February 1965, pp 138-144.
185	International Aerospace Abstracts: Application of microfiche in the field of science and technology. Microfiche Foundation Newsletter, Pt. 7, December 1964, page 2.
186	Clearinghouse for Federal Scientific and Technical Information bases report dissemination program on microfiche. Microcard Bulletin, number 30, January 1965, pp 1-4.
187	Kepple, R. R.: Microfiche utilisation at the International Atomic Energy Agency. Microfiche Foundation Newsletter No. 13, January 1967, pages 24-26.
188	Euratom (Brussels). Microfiche Newsletter (7), December 1964, page 2.
189	Pandex Promotional Literature on the Pandex Service. No date. Pandex, 135 West 50th Street, New York, N.Y. 10020.
190	Scheffel, W.: The present significance of Microfilm in the Federal Republic of Germany. NMA Proceedings, 12th annual meeting and convention 1963, pp 354-358.
192	Speeding Zip Coding; fast method to locate number. Plan and Print, May 1967, pp 26-28.
193	Micro-Zip Service. National Micro News, number 87, 1967, pp 180-181.
194	Microfilmed instruction manuals for airlines. Reproduction, Vol. 5, Pt. 1, January 1968, pp 4 and 6.
195	Riding, R. I.: Micro-Manuals. Aeroplane, Vol. 114, Pt. 2916, 6 September 1967, page 56.
196	American Airlines microfilm services plant and office. Systems, Vol. 8, Pt. 6, June 1967, pp 24 and 36.
197	Field Survey Note. No. 6. Visit from Mr. D. Mayer, CIBA. 4th May 1967. Hatfield College of Technology (Unpublished).
198	New automative aerospace data goes microfiche via SAE. TMC Report on Microfiche, October 1965.
199	Maynard, T. G.: Microfilm in the Graphic Arts. NMA Proceedings, 13th annual meeting and convention 1964, pp 287-296.
200	Clarke, G. R.: Distribution and retrieval of subject file information in the world-wide organisation of Arthur Anderson & Co., National Micro-News, Pt. 88, 1967, pp 207-208.
201	Martyn, J. Pandex: Index to the world's scientific and technical periodicals. New York Pandex 1967 (Review) Journal of Documentation 24 (1), March 1968, pp 73-75.
202	Santoro, F. W.: Time-to-Find. A Vital Element. Systems, Vol. 7, Pt. 5, May 1966, pp 39 and 57.
203	Christian, W. C.: V.S.M.F. stars in Microfilm Publishing; special projects and Visual Search Microfilm Files (V.S.M.F.) launched a whole new company into becoming one of the world's largest microfilm publishers. Systems Vol. 7, Pt. 10, October 1966, pp 12-15, 42 and 46.
204	General Electric Co.: A study on the application of microfilming to the production, distribution, use and retrieval of technical reports by J. T. Salisbury, 30 April 1965, DDC AD–615 800.
205	Camras, M.: Information Storage Density. Society of Photographic Scientists and Engineers, 1965. Symposium on photography in information and storage and retrieval, pp 44-63.
206	Bagg, T. C., and Stevens, M. E.: Information selection systems. Retrieving replica copies: a state-of-the-art report. United States National Bureau of Standards, 1961, 172 pages, bibliography.
207	Bourne, C. P.: Survey of the Utilisation of Mechanised Image Systems. NMA Proceedings, 12th annual meeting and convention 1963, pp 290-298.
208	Bourne, C. P.: Mechanised Micro-image Systems. Methods of Information Handling, Wiley, 1963, pp 200-214.
209	Baptie, A. L.: The present state of microfilming in the United States. (Translated from the German: Der derzeiteign stand des mikrofilms in den U.S.A.). Reprographie, Vol. 7, No. 1, 1967, page 3.
210	Herbert, E.: Information transfer. International Science and Technology, March 1966, pp 26-37 and 104-106.
211	Cole, W. A.: Information storage and retrieval with microfilm. Internationaler Kongress fuer Reprographie, 1st Cologne 14-19th October, 1963, papers edited by O. Helwich (published as "Reprographie"), Darmstadt, Helwich, 1964, pp 264-265.
212	Angel, H. E.: Microfilm Information Retrieval in the Federal Government Status and Potential. NMA Proceedings, 12th annual meeting and convention, 1963, pp 263-271.
213	U.S. Federal Council for Science and Technology, Committee on Scientific and Technical Information (COSATI) Recommendations for National Document Handling Systems in Science and Technology. PB168 267 AD624. 608 pages, November 1965. (Microfiche)

Serial No.	*Reference*
214	Williams, B. J. S.: Microforms in information retrieval and communication systems Aslib Proceedings, Vol. 19, Pt. 7, July 1967, pp 223-231.
215	Williams, B. J. S.: Microfilm for business retrieval systems. Business Systems and Equipment, January 1968, pp 34-36, 38.
216	O'Connor, J.: A possibly inexpensive attachment for a microfilm reader to permit synchronised co-ordinate searching. AD 415 214, also in Journal of Chemical Documentation, Vol. 3, 1963, pp 29-32.
217	O'Brien, and others: New Unit Record Handling Techniques, NMA Proceedings, 12th annual meeting and convention, 1963, pp 302-319.
218	Silverman, D.: A high density random retrieval information storage system. National Micro-News No. 78, October 1965, pp 70-81.
219	Stine, L. G.: Random retrieval of micro-image cards. NMA Proceedings, 13th annual meeting and convention, 1964, pp 135-147.
220	1,500 microfilm readers aid reservation system. Office Equipment and Methods, Vol. 14, Pt. 1, January 1968.
221	Larsen, P. W.: CRIS. The Command Retrieval Information System. NMA Proceedings, 1962, pp 41-49.
222	Eccetron: Rapid information retrieval. Measurement and Control, Vol. 2, Pt. 8, August 1963, pp 312-314.
223	Rapid information retrieval. Measurement and Control, Vol. 2, Pt. 8, pp 312-314.
224	FMA Inc. Filesearch System: General information manual. Los Angeles FMA Inc. (1965?).
225	FMA Inc. The FMA Filesearch System: A special purpose information processing system for information storage and retrieval. No date (1965?), 10 pages (promotional literature).
226	Microfilm IR System; FMA Filesearch. Information Retrieval Letter, Vol. 1, Pt. 7, November 1965, pp 1-5.
227	FMA Inc.: Information retrieval on computer; comparing study. No date (1965?), 23 pages.
228	Filmorex: Descriptive leaflet, no date, 2 pages.
229	Samain, J.: Filmorex; a new technique of electronic research for information and documentation (Eine Neue Technik elektronischer recherche fuer information und dokumentation), Nachrichten fuer Dokumentation, Vol. 9, No. 1, March 1958, pp 35-40. (In German.)
230	IBM United Kingdom Limited. IBM Photo-Image Retrieval System 1966 (promotional literature).
231	Jenkins, D. D.: Magnetic Indexing Microfilm Storage and Information Retrieval. NMA Proceedings, 11th annual meeting and convention 1962, pp 205-212.
232	—
233	Ruterbusch, M. J.: Micracode—A new breakthrough in Automated Information Retrieval. NMA Proceedings, 12th annual meeting and convention 1963, pp 321-329.
234	Daniel, —.: Solving Information Retrieval Problems with Micracode. Journal of Chemical Documentation, Vol. 6, Pt. 3, August 1966, pp 147-148.
235	Hayter, R.: Central encumbrance registry with fast look-up aids banks. Office Equipment and Methods, Vol. 14, Pt. 3, March 1968, pp 31-33, 79, 80.
236	Janda, K. Political Research with Miracode. NMA Journal, Vol. 1, Pt. 2, Winter 1968, pp 41-47. Also in Social Science Information, April/June 1963, pp 169-181.
237	Mueller-Saala, H.: Miracode, an electronic microfilm evaluation method. (Miracode Eing Elektronisches Verfahren zur Auswertung van Mirofilmen), Reprographie, Vol. 7, Pt. 2, 1967, pp 25 and 26. (In German.)
238	Campbell, R. C.: Alden/Miracode microfilm retrieval and communication system. National Micro-News, No. 84, 1966, pp 52-57.
239	Automatic retrieval of microfilm records. Data Processing, Vol. 5, May/June 1963, pp 132-133.
240	Pike, J. L., and Bagg, T. C.: The rapid selector and other NBS document retrieval studies. NMA Proceedings, 11th annual meeting and convention, 1962, pp 213-227.
241	Wise, C. S., and Perry, J. W.: Coding information retrieval and the rapid selector. American Documentation, Vol. 1, pt. 2, April 1950, pp 76-86.
242	Rapid document retrieval; the Mosler Selectriever. Reprographics, Vol. 5, Pt. 8, August 1967, pp 11-13.
243	Tyler, A. W., and others: The application of the Kodak Minicard system to problems of documentation. American Documentation, Vol. 6, Pt. 1, January 1955, pp 18-30.
244	Xerox Corporation. Final engineering report on the development of a Minicard viewer Processor . . .prepared for Rome Air Development Center. MX 1993 (XW-1)G. Final report, Rochester, New York: June 1961, 70 pages, AD260073 (microfiche).

Serial No.	Reference

245 Vogel, N. A.: Walnut Document Storage and Retrieval System. NMA Proceedings, 11th annual meeting and convention 1962, pp 27-39.

246 Carr, W. H.: Microfilming in Mapping Applications. NMA Proceedings, 11th annual meeting and convention 1962, pp 249-254.

247 Ryder, J. P., and Goodwald, J. P.: TMCL-70mm Slide retrieval, Display and Print-Out System. Society of Photographic Scientists and Engineers, U.S. 1965 Symposium on photography in information storage and retrieval. Proceedings, pp 24 and 25.

248 Miner, R. A.: Magnetic Tape: a new Microreproduction Tool. NMA Proceedings, 12th annual meeting and convention 1963, pp 107-116.

249 Miner, R. A.: Videofile Document Storage System. Plan and Print, May 1966, pp 31-35, 72.

250 Ampex Videofile System. Office Machine Guide (58), September 1967. pp 15-17.

251 Dolleck, S., and Mullendore, R. E.: Microfilm at the Census Bureau; 30 years experience points to dynamic future. National Micro News No. 87, 1967, pp 161-167.

252 McPherson, J. L., and Volk, M.: Fosdic Microfilm Problems and their Solutions. NMA Proceedings, 11th annual meeting and convention, 1962, pp 193-203.

253 Bosen, J. F.: Data Processing Machines in Climatology. Weatherwise, Vol. 15, Pt. 4, August 1962, pp 158-159, 163.

254 U.S. National Bureau of Standards. Fosdic IV reads microfilmed weather data for computer. National Micro-News, No. 85, 1966, pp 103-107.

255 Palasky, E. C.: Microfilmed punched cards rapidly converted to binary codes. Control Engineering, Vol. 40, Pt. 4, April, 1967, page 103.

256 Microfilm; the efficient way to handle output data; S-C 4400 document recorder and the Recordak "Miracode" system together constitute an efficient method of recording and retrieving computer generated data. Data Processing, Vol. 8, Jan./Feb. 1966, pp 38-43.

257 U.S. Bureau of Census: Fosdic (Film optional sensing device for input to computer) general description. 1961, 47 pages.

258 British Standards Institution. BS 4189: 1967. Specification for conventional typographical character for legibility tests (ISO test character) 8 pages).

259 ISO Recommendation R435: ISO conventional typographical character for legibility tests (ISO character).

260 British Standards Institution. BS 4210: Part 1: 1967. Specification for 35mm microcopying of engineering drawings and associated data. Part 1: recommended procedures, 20 pages.

261 National Microfilm Association. Basic standards, specifications of the Department of Defense engineering data micro-reproduction system. Annapolis, N.MA, 1967, 268 pages.

262 Mieze, K.: Microfilm technique; explanations of the draft standards (Mikrofilmtechnik; erlaeuterungen zu den Norm-Entwuerfen (June 1967) DIN 19052, Sheet 1, DIN 19052, Sheet 2), Reprographie, Vol. 7, Pt. 9, page 174.

263 Microfilm Association of Great Britain. Proposed Standard Specification for Microfiche (issue 3A), October 1965.

264 The United States of America Standards Institute, National Micronews, 83, 1966, pp 28-30.

265 National Microfilm Association. Drafting standards for microfilmed engineering drawings by W. J. Gallagher and C. E. Nelson. No date, 8 pages.

266 National Microfilm Association. Facsimile Microfilm Engineering Standards Committee, First Report.

267 Nelson, C. E.: IMC goal; world standards. IMC Journal, No. 1, Fall 1967, pp 12 and 13.

268 German Standards DIN 19052, Sheets 1 and 2. Microfilm technique; filming of engineering drawings, Sheet 1; general principles, Sheet 2. Coyping on 35mm for mechanical processing. (Translated from the German) Sheet 1, 3 pages; Sheet 2, 4 pages, 1967.

269 —

270 U.S. Patent Office Specification for an aperture card reader (assigned title—title page from copy missing), 11 pages and appendices. No date (circ 1966-67).

271 British Standards Institution. BS 308: 1964, Supplement No. 1 (1967). Engineering drawing practice. The preparation of drawings suitable for microfilming.

272 British Standards Institution. BS 677: Parts 1 and 2, 1958. Motion picture film. London, B.S.I., 1958.

273 British Standards Institution. BS 1193: 1961. Specification for sizes of sensitized materials for recording instruments. London, B.S.I., 1961.

274 Crabtree, J. I., and others: The removal of hypo and silver salts from photographic materials as affected by the composition of processing solutions. Journal of the Society of Motion Picture and Television Engineers, Vol. 41, Pt. 14, 1943, page 51.

275 Pope, C. I.: Determination of residual thiosulphate in processed film. Journal of research of the National Bureau of Standards, Vol. 67C, Pt. 3, July/September 1963, pp 237-245.

Serial No.	Reference
276	American Standards Association. PH4.8: 1958. American standard method for determining the thiosulphate content of processed black and white photographic film and plates. New York, A.S.A. Inc., 1958.
278	British Standards Institution. BS 4191: 1967. Specification for essential characteristics of 35mm microfilm reading apparatus, B.S.I. 1967, 7 pages.
279	American Standards Association. ASA PH1.37, 1964. Methods for determining the scratch resistance of processed microfilm.
280	Stevens, G. W. W.: Microphotography; photography and photofabrication at extreme resolution, 2nd edition, London, Chapman and Hall, 1968.
281	Suydam, W. S., and Skove, A.: Scratch resistance parameters of microfilm emulsions. Proceedings of the National Microfilm Association, 13th annual meeting and convention, 1964, pp 49-59.
282	Notley, N. T.: Flash processing for information retrieval. Society of Photographic Engineers and Scientists (U.S.A.). Symposium on Information Storage and Retrieval, 1965, pp 32-33.
283	U.S. Navy: Blemishes on processed roll negative microfilm. National Micro-News, No. 78, October 1965, pp 91-93.
284	Nelson, C. E.: Microfilm technology in engineering and related fields. New York, McGraw Hill, 1965.
285	Myers, W. C.: Photochromic micro-image; a new technique for data recording and data dissemination. The National Cash Register Co., 1964 (Technical publication 2596).
286	National Cash Register Co.: Perforated input microfilm specifications for PCMI microform system. Revision 1 March 1969, N.C.R., 10 pages.
287	PCMI's double first; engineers benefit from PCMI's first commercial breakthrough. Business Systems and Equipment, April 1968, page 31.
288	Clark, K. G.: Itek's radiation sensitive process. Repro Autumn, 1968, page 5.
289	Association Pour la Conservation et la Reproduction Photographique de la Presse. Aims and activities, 1963.
290	Anglo-American cataloguing rules; British text. London. The Library Association, 1967.
291	New York Public Library distributes microfilm Information Retrieval and Library Automation, Vol. 3, No. 4, September 1967, page 3.
292	Veaner, A. B.: Developments in the reproduction of library materials and graphic communications. Library Resources and Technical Services, Vol. 12, Pt. 2, Spring 1968, pp 203-214.
294	American Standards Association PH1.25-1956: Safety photographic film, specifications for
295	American Standards Association PH5.6-1961: 100 foot reels for processed microfilm; dimensions for
296	Sophar, G. J.: The determination of the legal facts and economic guide posts with respect to the dissemination of scientific and educational information as it is affected by copyright; a status report. American Documentation, Vol. 19, No. 3, July 1968, pp 317-321.
297	Goodwin, N.: Compulsory licensing of information copies. Society of Photographic Scientists and Engineers (U.S.A.). Symposium on photography in information storage and retrieval, 1965, pp 84-85.
298	Frank, O.: Mikrofilm—Aufnahmegerate und Mikrofilm-Aufnah memaschinen. Reprographie, Vol. 8, No. 5, 1968, pp 119-125.
299	Riding, R. I.: Microfilm in information work; a case study. Microdoc, Vol. 7, No. 2, 1968, pp 37-39.
300	Microfilm for a technical reference library. Reproduction, Vol. 5, No. 7, July 1968, pp 14 and 15.
301	Illinois, University of. Department of Computer Science. Report 203. Design concepts for an information resource center with an option of an attached automated laboratory, by B. H. McCormick and A. M. Richardson, 1966, 44 pages.
302	Pfeffer, H.: Aperture card system adopted by ICIREPAT. Microfiche Foundation Newsletter, No. 16, May 1968, page 20.
303	Richmond, P. A.: Pandex. Review in American Documentation, Vol. 19, No. 3, July 1968, pp 357-358.
304	Merritt, C. A.: A global information system, I.M.C. Jorunal, No. 4, Summer 1968, pp 8-10.
305	Taube, M.: Trends in microfilm applications today and tomorrow. National Microfilm Association Proceedings, 14th annual meeting and convention, 1965, pp 36-43.
306	Adelstein, P. Z.: Review of proposed U.S.A. standard for archival film on cellulose ester base. NMA Journal, Vol. 1, No. 2, Winter 1968, pp 66-76.
307	Kish, J. L.: The proposed microfiche standard. Data Systems News, Vol. 9, No. 12, July 1968, pp 19 and 27.

308 British Standard 850: 1955. Definition of cinematographic safety film.

309 Ardern, L. L.: J. B. Dancer microphotographs extent. Microdoc, Vol. 2. No. 4, 1968, pp 75-78.

310 Ardern, L. L.: J. B. Dancer, originator of microphotography. Library Association Records, Vol. 65, June 1963, page 229.

311 Mackay, N.: The hole in the Card. Minnesota, The 3M Co., 1966.

312 French Standard PNZ 43-030. Microfiche transparente de format 105 x 148 mm. AFNOR, 19 Rue de 4 Septembre, Paris 2eme.

313 PCMI microform system, the parts list service of the future. BMC Service News, No. 57, May 1969.

314 Smitzer, L. A.: The art of roll film look-up. NMA papers and seminar materials, 17th annual convention, Chicago, May 1968, pp 57-73.

315 Gray, S. B.: Aspects of the computer/microfilm interface, NMA Sessions papers and seminar materials, 17th annual convention, Chicago, May 1968. pp 79-84.

316 Ray, S. R.: Prospects and problems in designing image orientated information systems. University of Illinois, Proceedings of the 1967 Clinic on Library Applications and Data Processing, edited by D. E. Carroll, Illinois University, 1967, pp 8-28.

317 Encyclopaedia Britannica: UMF resource and research libraries. National Cash Register Co.: PCMI library information system. Microfiche Foundation Newsletter, No. 20, July 1969, pp 40 and 42.

318 Little pictures show big savings, part 2; filming the information explosion. Modern Office Procedures, Vol. 13, No. 6, June 1968, pp 36-45.

319 Hilton, H. J.: Identification and copyright; two problems in microform systems. NMA Session papers and seminar material, 17th convention, Chicago, May 1968, pp 151–1810

320 American Library Association. Library Technology Report: Manufacturers and makers of microform equipment, May 1968, 7 pages.

321 The American Society for Information Science. The National Auxiliary Publications Service (Promotional literature obtainable from the society at: 2000 P Street NW., Washington D.C. 20036.

322 Wooster, H.: Our nervous science publishers. The Torch, July 1968, pp 14, 28-32.

323 Prinet, J.: Presse microfilmee, le constitution de collections completes des journaux et de revues sur microfilms de long metrage. Internationaler Kongress fur Reprographie, Koln 14-19 Oktober 1963. Papers edited and published by O. Helwich. (Published as "Reprographie", Darmstadt 1964, pp 322-323.)

324 Spotlight on Mr. W. R. Hawken. Microfiche Foundation Newsletter, No. 17, August 1968, pp 1-4.

325 Leisinger, A. H.: Selected aspects of microreproduction in the United States National Archive Accessions, No. 60, December 1967, pp 29-49.

326 U.S. Patent 3,263,557. Document recording systems. R. Cunningham, assigner to the General Electric Co., 1966.

327 U.S. Patent 3,373,019. Method and apparatus for producing images. W. E. Bixby, assigner to the Bell & Howell Co., 1964.

328 Boone, J. W.: Current administrative practices in library photographic services; a thesis submitted to the . . . University of North Carolina . . . 1965, 81 pages. (ACRL Microcard series No. 151-2 micro-opaques).

329 Wooster, H.: Towards a uniform federal report numbering system and a 'cuddly' microfiche reader. NMA Journal, Vol. 2, No. 2, Winter 1968/69, pp 63-67.

330 Schatz, S.: Facsimile transmission in libraries; a state-of-the-art survey Library Resources and Technical Services, Vol. 12, No. 1, Winter 1968, pp 5-15.

331 Hilton, F. L.: Microfilm systems; the first Kodak 40 years. NMA Journal, Vol. 1, No. 4, Summer 1968, pp 117-125.

332 Meier, M. F.: RX for drug research, microfilm and MIS. Information and Records Management, Vol. 2, No. 4, April / May 1968, pp 49-51.

333 Ploscowe, A. W.: Centralised microfilm records cutting costs and speeding retrieval. Plan and Print, Vol. N42, No. 5, May 1969, pp 22-24, 38.

334 Kennington, D., and Adams, R. J.: Selecting the right microfilm trade data retrieval system. Electrical Review; Vol. 183, No. 12, September 1968, pp 417-419.

335 Southern Pacific Railroad files documents by television. Data Systems News, Vol. 9, No. 15, October 1968, pp 1 and 23.

336 Mark, K, and Funderburk, B. J.: Finding the needle in the haystack and putting it to work for progress. Data Systems News, Vol. 19, No. 15, October 1968, pp 20 and 21.

337 Weber, J. R.: Microfilm makes it easier to fly. Business Automation (International Edition), Vol. 15, No. 10, October 1968, pp 38-41.

Serial No.	*Reference*
338	Merritt, C. A.: The IBM Corporate program for technical documentation, NMA Journal, Vol. 1, No. 4, Summer 1968, pp 126-128.
339	Drattell, A.: Railroad pioneers with Videofile Business Automation (International edition), Vol. 15, No. 10, October 1968, pp 45-47.
340	Starker, L. N., and Kuney, J. H.: Microfilm costs (letters to the editor). Chemical and Engineering News, Vol. 45, No. 53, 18 December 1967, page 687.
341	The paradox of microduplication (editorial). The NRCd bulletin, Vol. 2, No. 3, Summer 1969, page 1.
342	Crow, J. E.: Microforms and technical information. Journal of Chemical Documentation, Vol. 8, No. 4, November 1968, pp 204-207.
343	Ardern, L. L.: John Dancer; father of microfilming. Reproduction, Vol. 6, No. 1, January 1969, page 26.
344	Teplitz, A.: Microfiche for technical information dissemination; a cost benefit analysis. Offprint 15 pages. No date (1968).
345	Ver Hulst, J.: An approach to the development of a large volume information dissemination system. NMA Journal, Vol. 2, No. 3, Spring 1969, pp 111-112.
346	Veaner, A. B.: The crisis in micropublication. Choice, Vol. 5, No. 4, June 1968, pp 448-453.
347	The New York Times on microfilm. Choice, Vol. 5, No. 10, December 1968, pp 1276-1279.
348	U.S. Patent 3,373,019. Method and apparatus for producing images. W. E. Bixby, assignor to the Bell & Howell Co. Filed May 1964.
349	Lenneberg, H.: Problems in the international exchange of microfilm. Fonts Artis Musicae, Vol. 15, No. 2-3, May-Dec. 1968, pp 75-82.
350	Kiesewetter, G. H.: Technical communications in a decentralised corporation. NMA Journal, Vol. 2, No. 2, Winter 1968/69, pp 40-43.
351	Judisch, J. M.: The effects of positive-negative microforms and front-rear projection on reading speed and comprehension. NMA Journal, Vol. 2, No. 2, Winter 1968/69, pp 58-61.
352	Microbook—breakthrough in retrieval? Business Systems and Equipment, June 1969, page 39.
353	Selective dissemination of microfiches (SDM). Clearinghouse Announcements in Science and Technology, 25 April 1969 (news item).
354	American Library Association. Library Technology Report. The Selection of a microform reader. November 1968, 19 pages.

AUTHOR, NAME AND TRADE NAME INDEX

Subject | *Page No.*

Subject	*Page No.*
need for improvements	38
noise from motors	52
numbers in use	69
personal	82, 135
positive/negative displays	28
rear projection	28, 52
screen materials	52
35mm roll	59
Readers, roll microfilm: compatibility with cameras	27
standards	59, 141
Reading, continuous: acceptance of microforms	58
Reading rooms: library systems	52–54
Reduction ratios: communications factors	62
NBS recommendations	58
optimum for libraries	56–59, 82
quality control	55 See also Scaling.
standards	56
Reels: standards	141
Reports: publication on microforms	90–94
Resolution: diazo films	17
frost xerography	21
Kalvar film	19
requirements of 6 point type	62
standard	55–60 See also:
terminology	8 legibility.
Test targets	141–142, 144
Retrieval	See: information retrieval.
Reviews of micropublications	44
Roll microfilms:	
costs of publishing on	77
packaged libraries	67
standards	56
16mm original publishing on	76
35mm original publishing on	76
manuals publications on	96–97
product information services published on	98–103
readers (evaluation)	135
report publishing on	93
speed of access with cassettes/reels (disadvantages)	26
standards	56, 57, 60, 141, 144
Scaling targets: standards	56 (See also: Reduction ratios).
Scratch resistance: diazo films	17
silver halide films	15
Screen materials: reading room design	52
Scrolls: information retrieval	116
SDI	(See: selective dissemination of information).